George I. Wright

Elements of Civil Government

Prepared for the Public Schools of Pennsylvania

George I. Wright

Elements of Civil Government
Prepared for the Public Schools of Pennsylvania

ISBN/EAN: 9783337119607

Printed in Europe, USA, Canada, Australia, Japan

Cover: Foto ©Suzi / pixelio.de

More available books at **www.hansebooks.com**

OF

CIVIL GOVERNMENT

PREPARED FOR

THE PUBLIC SCHOOLS OF PENNSYLVANIA

BY

GEORGE I. WRIGHT, Ph.D.,

Superintendent of Schools of Crawford County, Penn'a.

MEADVILLE, PA.:
PUBLISHED BY THE AUTHOR.

PREFACE.

The need for some elementary instruction in our common schools, on the duties and responsibilities of citizenship, has long impressed me as of much importance; and in looking over the field to see if some logical, and at the same time elementary, guide could be found, I have failed to find what I wanted. As a school man, interested more particularly in the great body of common schools, the schools which educate the masses, I feel that an effort is warranted to simplify, and adapt to the uses of such schools, the explanation of those principles of government which should be known to every intelligent citizen. It seems to me that the logical method would be to begin at home, with the lowly official duties which touch the local government of communities. Hence this effort to furnish to my teachers some guide to help them to follow out instructions along this line. This is my only excuse for the publication of the following pages.

I have made free to use what I needed, from any source, and I here take pleasure in acknowledging my indebtedness to all from whom such aid was obtained.

G. I. WRIGHT.

Meadville, Pa., December 1, 1893.

CONTENTS.

PART I.—GENERAL PRINCIPLES.

CHAPTER.		PAGE.
I.	CIVIL SOCIETY	9
II.	GOVERNMENTS	11
III.	RIGHTS	12
IV.	LIBERTY	14

PART II.—TOWNSHIPS AND TOWNSHIP AFFAIRS.

V.	GENERAL REMARKS	16
VI.	SCHOOL DISTRICTS	17
VII.	SCHOOL DIRECTORS	18
VIII.	LOCAL AND TOWNSHIP ELECTIONS	19
IX.	TOWNSHIP OFFICERS—JUSTICES OF THE PEACE—CONSTABLE—AUDITORS—ASSESSOR	21
X.	TOWNSHIP OFFICERS (Con.)—COLLECTOR—JUDGE OF ELECTIONS—INSPECTORS OF ELECTION—SCHOOL DIRECTORS	22
XI.	TOWNSHIP OFFICERS (Con.)—TOWNSHIP CLERK—TREASURER—OVERSEERS OF THE POOR—PATHMASTERS	24
XII.	VILLAGES, TOWNS AND CITIES	27

PART III.—COUNTY AND COUNTY AFFAIRS.

XIII.	HISTORICAL	30

CONTENTS.

XIV.	COUNTY ELECTIONS . . .	32
XV.	COUNTY COURTS—COMMON PLEAS COURT--ORPHANS' COURT--COURT OF QUARTER SESSIONS OF THE PEACE—COURT OF OYER AND TERMINER AND GENERAL JAIL DELIVERY—LICENSE COURT .	33
XVI.	COUNTY OFFICERS — SHERIFF— COUNTY CORONER — COUNTY SURVEYOR	35
XVII.	COUNTY OFFICERS (Con.)—DISTRICT ATTORNEY—CLERK OF COURTS— PROTHONOTARY — REGISTER OF WILLS—RECORDER OF DEEDS— COUNTY COMMISSIONERS . .	37
XVIII.	COUNTY OFFICERS (Con.)—COUNTY TREASURER — AUDITORS — JURY COMMISSIONERS— POOR DIRECTORS — COUNTY SUPERINTENDENT OF SCHOOLS	39

PART IV.—THE STATE.

XIX.	HISTORICAL	42
XX.	THE LEGISLATURE . . .	43
XXI.	EXECUTIVE OFFICERS—GOVERNOR— LIEUTENANT·GOVERNOR — STATE TREASURER—AUDITOR GENERAL SECRETARY OF INTERNAL AFFAIRS	44
XXII.	EXECUTIVE OFFICERS (Con.)— SECRETARY OF THE COMMONWEALTH—ATTORNEY GENERAL— SUPERINTENDENT OF PUBLIC INSTRUCTION—ADJUTANT GENERAL —INSURANCE COMMISSIONER .	46

XXIII.	THE STATE JUDICIARY	48

PART V.—THE NATION.

XXIV.	HISTORICAL	50
XXV.	LEGISLATIVE DEPARTMENT	52
XXVI.	LEGISLATIVE DEPARTMENT (CON.)	53
XXVII.	EXECUTIVE DEPARTMENT—PRESIDENT	55
XXVIII.	EXECUTIVE DEPARTMENT (CON.)—VICE-PRESIDENT—SECRETARY OF STATE–SECRETARY OF THE TREASURY — SECRETARY OF WAR — SECRETARY OF NAVY — SECRETARY OF THE INTERIOR—POSTMASTER GENERAL — ATTORNEY-GENERAL—SECRETARY OF AGRICULTURE	57
XXIX.	JUDICIAL DEPARTMENT	59
XXX.	THE NATION	61
DECLARATION OF INDEPENDENCE.		66
ARTICLES OF CONFEDERATION		72
PART OF THE ORDINANCE OF 1787		84
CONSTITUTION OF THE UNITED STATES		88
CONSTITUTION OF PENNSYLVANIA		110
APPENDIX		159

ELEMENTS OF CIVIL GOVERNMENT.

PART I.
GENERAL PRINCIPLES.

CHAPTER I.
CIVIL SOCIETY.

Men cannot exist and reach the highest development, either as individuals or as a race, unless they associate themselves together. They are fitted naturally to associate with each other, each being dependent for many things on his fellow-men. The solitary state is impossible. Should we consider the family as the unit, it would still be impossible to get along without some sort of arrangement by which people could help one another. Hence, men live together in a social state, which is called civil society.

Men are not always just to one another. Some are disposed to do things which would defraud or injure those with whom they are associated. Some would steal or, perhaps, murder, others would do all manner of wrong, so that civil society itself could not exist without some rules of action laid down for the guidance of men in their social relations. Such rules are called laws. Laws, to be of any use, must have some power back of them to enforce them. Hence the necessity for some form of government.

THE STATE, which is but another name for civil society, cannot exist for any length of time without government. Occasionally, when, from one cause or another, people become turbulent and overturn the existing government, and fail for a time to substitute another in its place, we have social disorder, or what is known as anarchy. But society, or the state, for the protection of its individual members, soon erects among the ruins of the discarded government, some new and often better form of government. Government, then, is necessary to make and enforce the rules of action, or laws, by which men are compelled to be just to one another.

The power resides in the state, that is, in the people considered collectively, and not in the government, which is but the agent of society, for securing to all men justice. All laws should be just laws, since justice is the fundamental idea on which the state, or civil society, was organized. Since society gives to government all its powers, these powers should be used for the benefit of the people. Government, then, is constituted for the purpose of protecting society and securing to the individual members thereof that liberty or freedom which is in harmony with the principle of justice which underlies the whole scheme.

CHAPTER II.

GOVERNMENTS.

Governments are of various kinds, and that is best which, under all conditions, is best adapted to secure the ends for which it is established, that is, equal rights and justice to all men. The form which would best suit the conditions and circumstances under which civil society was organized in one section, might not be the best under other and different conditions. Hence we have the absolute monarchy in one place, under one set of conditions, and the limited monarchy in another place and under a different set of conditions, and a republic under still different conditions. The common forms are: monarchy, aristocracy, and democracy.

Monarchies are either absolute or limited. A government in which society has placed all the power in the hands of one person, is called an absolute monarchy. One in which the power of the ruler is limited by laws, or by a constitution, or by any other power, is called a limited monarchy. All monarchies at present in existence are hereditary, that is, the nearest heir succeeds to the crown. In elective monarchies, the successor was elected by the people or their representatives whenever the monarch died. None such at present exists, and this fact may be said to prove that the elective form was less desirable than the hereditary.

In an aristocracy the power is exercised by a few

persons, distinguished either for their rank or their wealth. At present, this form of government does not exist, though the principle is found in such bodies as the House of Lords in the British government.

Democracy is government by the people. Pure democracy is not possible, except in small communities, where it is possible for all the people to assemble. Hence, at present, there are none.

The republic is the nearest approach to pure democracy at present possible. In this form of government, the power to make and execute laws for society rests in representatives elected by the people. In such a government the people not only say who shall act for them, but they adopt a code of general laws called a constitution, which is superior to all other laws, and under which their representatives must act.

CHAPTER III.

RIGHTS.

The individual members of society have certain rights which are called natural or civil rights; natural, because given by nature; civil, because they relate to the duties of all citizens. These are the right to security in life, health and reputation, the right to go where they choose, the right to acquire and enjoy property, the right to protection of government, and the right to family relations of husband and wife, parent and child, etc.

Then there are political rights, but all people composing civil socjety do not possess them. In an absolute monarchy, society relinquishes all the political rights of its individual members, such as the right to have a voice in the government or in the selection of the rulers. In all other forms of government that exist to-day, the people have some political rights. The right to vote is a political right, though some think it should be a natural right, "an attribute of humanity," in which case women and children would have the same right to this privilege that men have. Many think that the right to vote on all subjects which concern society, should be given to all people who are subject to law, without regard to sex or condition. But, since the state is under obligation to give its people the best possible form of government, it is under obligations to use the means considered best adapted to secure the end sought, and if, under all circumstances, a restricted suffrage will give the best rulers and lawmakers, then the right to vote should be restricted to those most competent to give to society such rulers and such lawmakers. But if universal suffrage is most likely to secure the desired end, then all people who are subject to law and are of sound and mature mind should be allowed to have a voice in choosing those officers who are to rule over them. The tendency during the past ages has been to extend this privilege first to one class of citizens, then to another, until now, in many places, all men, without regard to rank or condition, as well as women, are given a voice in public affairs. If this extension of the political rights of the citizen proves satisfactory where it is tried, there is no reason why it should not be extended everywhere.

CHAPTER IV.

Liberty.

Liberty is the freedom to exercise and enjoy our rights. "Liberty is the result of law,—not as some suppose, of the absence of law. Many think that people are free only as they are without restraint, and feel that in so far as they are under law they are without liberty." Such is not the case, however, since law is designed to give to all people security, protection, and all the liberty they can lawfully claim. People have no right to murder, or to steal, or to do wrong; hence laws which forbid these things do not abridge their liberty. People have no right to do things which are contrary to the best interests and to the welfare of society. Dr. Alden says: "A perfectly just and wise system of laws would forbid everything that is unjust in society, everything socially wrong, and would permit everything just in society, everything socially right. If such a system were carried into perfect execution, it would furnish perfect security against wrong, and perfect liberty to do right. The perfection of law and execution would secure the perfection of liberty." "Security against wrong, and not the transient absence of wrong, is the essential of liberty."

PART II.

TOWNSHIPS AND TOWNSHIP AFFAIRS.

CHAPTER V.

General Remarks.

"The American citizen lives under not less than five institutions called governments. He is a member of a school district. He is a member of a civil township, a town, or city government. He is a part of a county government. He is ruled over by a State government. He is also under a federal, general, or national government."—*Macy*. "Each performs separate, special work, for the good of the people, and all are more or less closely connected with one another."

In these United States, the State represents organized civil society, as the governmental unit. The federal government exercises certain powers, which have been given up to it by the States; powers which concern the welfare of all the citizens of the entire country. The minor divisions of the State—school district, township, and county,—exercise only such powers as are permitted by the State, and in all things are governed by laws enacted by the State legislature.

The township, as here used, means the local division of the county. In some States it is called town, as in New England, in others parish, as in some of the Southern States, but in most States it is called township. Wherever the government system of land survey has been followed it is six miles square, and is divided into squares, with roads regularly laid out. In Pennsylvania they are irregular in size and shape and were arbitrarily laid out for the convenience of the electors in getting to a prescribed voting place. Boundaries are usually determined either by streams, which at times might be impassable, or by the irregular roads which were made from settlement to settlement or from farm to farm, by the early settlers.

CHAPTER VI.

School Districts.

School districts, as here used, are the areas under separate local school governments. In some States each school has a separate local government, as in Ohio. In other States the several schools of a township constitute a school district.

In Pennsylvania the township or boro is the general school area, except where special areas are allowed, as independent districts, where the people want, and are willing to pay for, better school privileges than are afforded by the general township board. In these cases, boundaries are established by order of court, and a separate government allowed.

In 1787 Congress passed an ordinance by which, in the territory west of Pennsylvania and north of the Ohio River, including all land ceded to the general government by the several States or colonies, and all that should thereafter come into the possession of the United States, every sixteenth section of land should be sold for the benefit of the schools. This gave a fund which, in nearly all of the Western States helps to support the public schools.

In the Western States, where the country is laid out in sections, a schoolhouse is usually located every two miles on alternate roads, in the center of each four sections, so that no child ever has more than two miles to walk, which is considered as far as any one should be required to go.

Whatever form of local school government is adopted, the single school system, the mixed system, or the township system, the work done by the local board is nearly the same.

CHAPTER VII.

SCHOOL DIRECTORS.

School directors are township or boro officers to whom are committed the educational interests of the district. In Pennsylvania the board consists of six members (except in cities), one third of whom are elected annually, making the term of office three years. The school year begins on the first Monday of June, when the old board settles its affairs, makes its reports, and adjourns; then the new board organizes, newly elected men are sworn in and officers elected, which are president, secretary, and treasurer. School directors are not paid officers, except that the secretary and treasurer may be paid for their special services. Their duty is to make the tax levy (which in some States is done by a county board, in others by a vote of the citizens), repair and build houses as it becomes necessary, fix the length of the school term, the wages of teachers, hire teachers, procure supplies (including text-books), and do all other things necessary to the best interests of the schools. The funds for the support of the schools in Pennsylvania are received from two sources: a local tax, varying from one half a mill to 26 mills (13 mills for school purposes and 13 mills for building purposes), and an appropriation from State funds, of not less than one million dollars, which the State Constitution orders, and which may be increased at the discretion of the State legislature, but cannot be diminished. At present (1893) it is five million dollars, five and a half million dollars for the years 1894 and 1895.

CHAPTER VIII.

LOCAL OR TOWNSHIP ELECTIONS.

Local elections are usually held in the spring of each year, the time varying in different States. In

Pennsylvania these elections are held on the third Tuesday of February. On the morning of this day the election officers open the polls, or voting places, and are ready to receive the votes of the qualified electors. In most States what is known as the Australian Ballot System, or some modification of it, is now used.

This system is designed to give a certain degree of privacy to the voter while he is making up his ballot, the printed form of which is furnished by the proper authorities.

The election house or booth is divided into stalls with a shelf on which to write, and a pencil for marking the ballot. The voters take their places in the stalls and mark the ballots as they wish to vote them, free from the surveillance or watching of interested parties. It is believed that this system tends to purify the elections from the influence of men and money, since people are not so apt to pay money for votes when they have no way of seeing that they get what they pay for. The venal and unlawful use of money had become so common that elections were often carried by this means, and men, no matter how competent, who had not money to pay for the votes, had no chance of being chosen. This state of affairs led to the adoption of this system of voting in nearly all the States of the Union. It is used in township, county, State, and national elections. In Pennsylvania the law is known as the "Baker Ballot Law," a modification of the Australian system.

CHAPTER IX.

Township Officers.

The officers chosen at the township election are: Two justices of the peace, one constable, three auditors, one assessor, one collector, one judge of elections, two inspectors of elections, six school directors, three supervisors, one clerk, and one treasurer.

Justices of the Peace are chosen for five years. They preside over justice courts, which are the lowest courts in the land, and the ones on which all others are founded. The justice hears and decides suits of every description growing out of disputes which continually arise in society. Petty offenses, and suits involving small amounts, usually under the value of $100, are tried here, though in all cases there is an appeal to the higher courts. Justices may perform the marriage ceremony. Their salaries consist of fees charged for services and collected of the parties to the suits. In cities justices are called magistrates.

The Constable is elected for three years. He is commissioned by the court and is responsible for the peace of the community. He executes the orders of the justice of the peace, and when acting by order of the court his authority is supreme; if he is resisted he can call upon any citizen or citizens to assist him. For his services he receives fees fixed by law, varying with different kinds of service.

The Auditors are elected for three years, one new one each year. The duties of the board of auditors are to examine the books and vouchers of the various officers who have charge of township money, as treasurers for the board of supervisors, and school board. They certify to the correctness of the accounts and publish annually a statement setting forth the receipts and expenditures of public money. They are paid $2.00 a day out of town money by the supervisors for their services.

The Assessor, with two assistants each third year, is elected for three years. His duty is to examine and fix values on all taxable property (land, horses, cattle, dogs, money, etc.) found within the township. This valuation is made according to the best judgment of the assessor, but people who are not satisfied can appeal to the commissioners, who act as a court of appeal in this matter. All electors whose occupation tax does not amount to $1.00 are assessed what is called a minimum occupation tax of $1.00, which is added to the school tax. Assessors and their assistants are paid $2.00 a day for their services, out of township funds, by the supervisors.

CHAPTER X.

TOWNSHIP OFFICERS (Continued).

The Collector is elected for one year, and gives bonds to the commissioners for the faithful performance of his duties. His term of office begins the first Monday of April. In Pennsylvania he has three kinds of tax to collect, a separate duplicate being furnished for each. The duplicate is a book having the names of all taxables in the township, with the valuation of property as given by the assessors. One of these duplicates is given out by the supervisors, in which the cash road tax is figured out as soon as the rate of levy for that purpose is made, which is usually early in April. Another is given out by the school board, as soon as the new board organizes in June, and the levy for school purposes is made. Still another is given him early in April, by the county commissioners, as soon as they make out the levy for State, county, and poor purposes. In this duplicate is also put the tax on dogs. The collector, we see, serves both the township and county. He is one of the most important of the township officers. He receives as pay for his services, two per cent on all taxes paid to him within sixty days of the date of his printed or posted notice, and five per cent on all paid after the expiration of the sixty days.

The Judge of Elections is elected for one year. It is his duty to decide all disputes in regard to the qualifications of those offering to vote. He also acts as return judge, that is, he carries the results to the proper place for recording, usually the county seat. He receives $1.50 a day for his services, and mileage in addition for services as return judge.

The Inspectors of Election are elected for one year. These inspectors shall be of different political parties, each elector voting for one inspector. The two receiving the highest number of votes are elected. It is their duty to keep the record of the voters, and assist the judges of election in all matters pertaining to the election. They appoint clerks to keep the tally-sheets, and each inspector, as well as the clerks, receives $1.50 a day for his services.

Two *School Directors* are elected each year, for three years, whose duties, etc., are set forth under the head of School Districts, Chapter IV.

CHAPTER XI.

Township Officers (Continued).

Three supervisors are elected, one each year, to serve three years. This number may be increased by vote of a majority of electors ; when increased, the term changes, if four are elected then two are elected each year to serve two years. The auditors shall require supervisors to give bonds. The compensation received by supervisors is $1.50 a day for time spent in performing the several duties of the office. It is the business of the supervisors to look after the public highways and care for them. They levy the road tax, both cash and work tax ; they appoint the path-masters, see to the erection and repair of township bridges, purchase and care for the road machines and other tools belonging to the township; they also have charge of all township buildings, election houses and the like. No more important local officers are elected by the people than supervisors.

The public highways of our own country are much inferior to those of other countries, and yet a vast amount of money is collected each year in the form of road tax, and annually expended upon the highways, but is used in such a desultory and unscientific way that it is for the most part wasted. After from fifty to a hundred years of this kind of road-making; after the expenditure of money and labor enough to have paved or macadamized the principal roads of the land, the people of the country and many towns are obliged to wade through mud and mire for the larger part of the year, many of the highways becoming actually impassable. It is high time that some reform be made in this matter, and the officers who are empowered to tax people for this purpose be held to stricter accountability for the manner in which the people's money is used. Hence we see that supervisors should be carefully selected, and then upheld by public sentiment in the right and scientific building and repair of roads.

The Township Clerk is elected each year for one year. It is his duty to keep a record of the proceedings of the board of supervisors. He draws all orders on the township treasurer, serves notices, and performs any other public duties ordered by the board of supervisors. He is paid such compensation for his services as the board of supervisors shall determine.

The Treasurer is elected for one year, and it is his duty to give bond to the supervisors, to take charge of all money collected on duplicates issued by this board—that is, road tax or received from any other source, and to pay out the same on orders signed by the board and attested by the clerk. He receives for his services a certain per cent of money expended: the rate is fixed by supervisors, with approbation of the auditors. He must keep an accurate account of the money received and expended and lay the same before the board of auditors.

Overseers of the Poor.—Townships in counties having no poorhouses managed by the county commissioners, or poor districts with poorhouses managed by directors of the poor, shall elect two overseers of the poor, one each year, to serve two years, such officers to receive $1.00 a day for services rendered.

Pathmasters are men appointed by the board of supervisors, whose duty it is to look after certain sections of road called "beats." To such is given a book containing the names, and amount of tax against each taxable belonging to his beat, and it is his duty to notify these persons when he wants them to come and work out the road tax against them. For his services he receives credit on his own work tax at the rate of $1.50 a day.

CHAPTER XII.

Villages, Towns, and Cities.

A village is generally a small collection of dwellings, though in some States the name is given to quite large business centers. In most States villages are not incorporated, that is, are not given by special legislation territorial limits and a new local government. In many States the word town is used in the same sense, though in general this name is given to a larger collection of buildings, and one that is incorporated, that is, has a charter and its own local government. In Pennsylvania such villages or towns are called boroughs. A borough has its deed of incorporation granted by the State legislature, either by special or general law. It is made a distinct political community, its privileges are enumerated, its officers have their duties assigned them, and it is empowered like the township to act independently, though under the State and national Constitutions.

A city always has a special local government, differing but slightly from that of boroughs or incorporated towns. In some States there are cities with less than 1,000 inhabitants, while in others there are villages or towns with 15,000 inhabitants, and yet having the simplest form of local government.

City government usually conforms to our general governmental scheme in having an executive called the mayor, a legislative body called a council or board of aldermen, and a judicial department which consists of police or magistrate courts, in place of the usual justice courts of townships, though in some cities they are exactly like the ordinary justice court. The council is often composed of two bodies, a common and a select council.

The other city officials differ little except in name from the corresponding township officers. Instead of constable they have chief of police and policemen; instead of supervisors they have street commissioners; they have auditors, assessors, collectors of taxes, and treasurers. Then they have special officers not needed in country communities, such as city solicitor, city superintendent of schools (elected by the school board), besides boards of health, fire commissioners, etc., usually appointed by the executive officer.

For convenience of organization and government, cities are usually divided off into wards, and in large cities wards are divided into precincts. Cities have larger demands for funds than country communities, hence, besides bearing a proportional share of general burdens of taxation by the county, they have special forms of taxation, such as assessments for paving and sidewalks, usually laid on adjoining property. License fees are collected from those dealing in liquor. Gas and water companies usually pay the city for their privileges; street car companies usually pay for the use of the streets, etc. Some cities own and operate the gas, water, and electric plants, charging the citizens for the use of the same, which makes these sources of revenue, and helps to lighten the otherwise heavy burden of taxation.

PART III.

COUNTY AND COUNTY AFFAIRS.

CHAPTER XIII.

HISTORICAL.

In England, where we found the type from which most of our local divisions are derived, the territory governed by a count was called a county, hence the name. These divisions were often called shires, the chief officer of which was called shire-reeve or sheriff, from which we have the name of our own local county officer though the duties have been much changed. In the South the county is the local unit. In New England the county is made up of "towns," and was first established for judicial purposes. Its functions have been extended, however, until now it exercises many which formerly belonged to the town. In New York, Pennsylvania, and other States west, we find the best types of organization. "Where the township exists, usually the county takes no more than local administration of justice, maintenance of county buildings, equalization of taxes, granting of certain licenses, and partial supervision of highways."—*Higby*.

Parish is the name given in Louisiana to this local area.

The New York form of township-county organization has been reproduced in many States farther west, as Michigan, Illinois, Wisconsin, and Nebraska. Under this form there is an executive board called the board of supervisors, composed of one supervisor from each township, who is at once a township and a county officer. They have the town meetings to legislate on certain matters, while the administrative county board, composed of township representatives, has general supervision. This system facilitates the shifting of business from one to the other as convenience may dictate.

In Pennsylvania the county was the first organized local unit; the Court of Quarter Sessions was the governing body, but the non-judicial business was taken out of the hands of the court and vested in a board of commissioners elected by the people of the county. Then the townships were organized for the purpose of choosing the local officers, some of whom we have seen act as agents for the county. In some places the townships care for the poor; in others the county maintains a poorhouse and farm, and takes charge of those who are so unfortunate as to need the help of their fellow-men in old age or misfortune and affliction. Here we have no town meeting with local legislative powers, this function being vested in the township board of supervisors. Modified forms of this system are found in Ohio, Indiana,

Iowa, and other States in this belt. Before the Civil War the Virginia type was found throughout the South, coextensive with slavery. These followed the model of the English shire Court of Quarter Sessions composed of justices originally appointed by the Governor, but afterwards nominated by the court itself, making it virtually a corporation filling its own vacancies. Here, then, only State officers were chosen by the people. Since the war, county commissioners have been elected, taking non-judicial business from this court, and the townships are beginning to appear as the people demand closer local supervision. The mixed system, as shown in New York or Pennsylvania, seems to give the people the largest possible share in local government, consistent with reasonable dispatch in the conduct of business.

CHAPTER XIV.

County Elections.

It is a nearly uniform custom to hold the elections for county officers on the first Tuesday after the first Monday of November. In some States such elections are held each year, but in Pennsylvania every three years, so that the term of office of all county officers (except judges) is three years, and they take possession of their respective offices the first of January next succeeding their election. These elections are conducted by the regularly elected local election officers, in the same manner and subject to the same laws and regulations as township elections. The regular county officers so elected are : judge, sheriff, coroner, prothonotary, clerk of courts, register of wills, recorder of deeds, and district attorney. These are all closely related to the judicial side of our local government. Three county commissioners (in some States called supervisors), three auditors, two jury commissioners, county surveyor, county treasurer, and county superintendent of schools.

The Governor appoints notaries public for three years, and the commissioners appoint their clerk and attorney, physician for the jail and poor, janitor for the courthouse, mercantile appraiser, and overseer of the poorhouse and farm.

CHAPTER XV.

County Courts.

President judge is in some senses the highest and most important officer in the county. He is elected by the people and serves for ten years, at a salary ranging from $4,000 to $7,000 a year, varying according to the amount of business to be transacted. The judge is commissioned by the Governor, and receives his pay also from the State treasury. At present in Pennsylvania, a judge is to be a man "learned in law." He presides over all the different kinds of county courts. In some States there are different judges for the different kinds of business. Sometimes the territory called judicial district, over which a judge holds court, is greater than the county, and sometimes less, as in large cities like Philadelphia and Pittsburg. So the judge is not, strictly speaking, a county officer, but is classed as such for convenience.

These courts are named Common Pleas Court, Orphans' Court, Court of Quarter Sessions, and Court of Oyer and Terminer.

In *Common Pleas Court* are tried all causes which grow out of breaches of contract, and the like. These are called civil cases.

Orphans' Court, in some States called *Probate Court* (with a special judge), hears all matters relating to the settlement of estates, wills, appointment of guardians, etc., which cannot be settled by the register of wills.

Court of Quarter Sessions of the Peace hears all causes of a criminal character, except such as are named in the law as coming under the jurisdiction of the higher criminal court.

The Court of Oyer and Terminer and General Jail Delivery tries all higher criminal cases, such as treason, murder, robbery, arson, and the like. In these cases, this court has exclusive jurisdiction, while it also tries certain kinds of criminal cases sent up by the Court of Quarter Sessions.

The judge also holds a special court called *License*

Court, in which are heard the claims of persons who apply for licenses to sell liquors.

Courts convene, usually, four times a year, beginning on the second Monday of January or February, and the session continues until the docket is cleared, or the judge adjourns court. The second session usually convenes on the second Monday of May, and is called the May term. The third session is set for the second Monday of September, and is called the September term, while the last term is called the November term. Where the same judge presides at all these courts, he can hear common pleas or criminal cases at any time, at his pleasure.

CHAPTER XVI.

County Officers.

The Sheriff is the guardian of the peace of the county, and executes the orders of the courts. He is elected at a general election of county officers, for three years, and cannot succeed himself. His compensation is paid in the form of fees, which are collected from the parties having business with him, and are fixed by law in the same manner as that of constable. He can execute the decrees of the court in any other county, but may not go into another State for this purpose except by permission of the Governor thereof. He seizes the property of delinquent debtors on order from the court and sells the same. From the proceeds of the sale he deducts the debt and the expenses of the sale, and returns to the owner of the property any balance there may be. He serves all papers of the court, has the care of county prisons and prisoners. He issues election proclamations, and must maintain the peace of the county, and if necessary may summon the *posse comitatus*, and in extreme cases call on the Governor and President for militia or military assistance. Such a case was that of the riot at Homestead in 1892, when several regiments were ordered out to keep the peace. From the nature of the business he often has large sums of money in his possession, in consequence of which he is required to give heavy bonds to the court for the faithful performance of his duty. His salary is either a fixed salary or a certain percentage, or fees as before stated. His office must be at the county seat.

The County Coroner is an officer elected for three years, whose duty is to hold inquisition, or "corooner's inquest," over the body of any person who has died a violent death, or who died while a prisoner. He summons a jury of bystanders to assist, called the coroner's jury. His duties are of considerable importance to society. He serves as sheriff in cases where the regular officer is a party, and in case of death or otherwise he becomes sheriff. Compensation consists of fees fixed by law. In cities the coroner is paid a salary ranging from $500 to $5,000 a year.

County Surveyor is also elected for three years. His duties vary in different States ; in some he has general charge of all road and bridge work, but in Pennsylvania the office is unimportant, and has to do only with the determining of boundaries, etc., when employed by private individuals.

CHAPTER XVII.

County Officers (Continued).

The District Attorney is elected for three years, at the general election. It is his duty to prosecute all persons charged with crime or offense against the law, who are brought before the court for trial. He acts for the county in all cases in which its interests are affected, unless the county commissioners have an attorney of their own. His compensation is made up of fees fixed by law, and is paid by the parties as assessed by the court or juries, or in default, by the county.

The Clerk of Courts is the recording officer of the court. He also is elected for three years. He keeps the records of business of the court and issues most of the legal papers used in the trial of causes. His seal proves the genuineness of any legal paper. His salary consists of certain fees collected for the issuance of legal papers, etc.

The Prothonotary is the clerk of the common pleas court. This is also an office of record. He issues all summonses and other processes in civil actions, enters all decrees of the court and issues all executions for their enforcement. All judgments are recorded here. He is paid by means of fees fixed by law.

The Register of Wills performs many of the duties of a probate court, takes all initiatory steps in the settlement of estates, recording of wills, and appointment of administrators and the like. In such matters he is not subject to the Orphans' Court, which has reference to final settlements, appointment of guardians, and the like. He is elected for three years, and is paid by fees collected of parties having business with him.

The Recorder of Deeds has charge of all records of the transfers of real estate, copies all deeds and mortgages, and keeps a permanent record of the same. The pay for this is collected of the parties doing business there, in the form of fees. In some counties, one person performs the functions of both offices.

The County Commissioners are the administrative officers of the county. The board consists of three members. They are elected for three years, and one of them must be the minority candidate who receives the highest number of votes. They have charge of county bridges, buildings, and other property. They levy taxes for State, county, and poor purposes, act as a board of equalization, have care of the county poor, provide voting places, and attend to all matters in which the county as a whole is interested. They appoint a clerk to the board, janitor to the court-house, an attorney to advise them in legal matters, an overseer of the poorhouse and farm, physician to the jail, mercantile appraiser, fix their salary, and make provision for their payment. They issue all orders on the county treasurer for money, approve the bonds of the treasurer and collectors, etc. They are paid $3.50 a day and actual traveling expenses, for services in both capacities as commissioners and overseers of the poor, out of the funds of the county. In some counties they are paid salaries fixed by special laws.

CHAPTER XVIII.

COUNTY OFFICERS (Continued).

The County Treasurer is elected for three years, and is ineligible for re-election to succeed himself. He gives bonds to the commissioners, and has charge of all State and county money. The former is paid out on warrant from the State treasurer, the latter on warrant from the county commissioners. He is paid a certain rate per cent on money paid out —rate fixed by county commissioners.

The Auditors are elected for three years, in the same manner as the county commissioners. The board consists of three members, one of whom is a minority candidate. The duties are to examine and pass upon all expenditures made by the board of commissioners. The report or statement of this board is published for the inspection of the people of the county.

Jury Commissioners are elected for three years, and receive $2.50 a day for their services. They, together with the judge, make up the lists of jurors from which the various juries are drawn. They have charge of the jury wheel, a device used in Pennsylvania for the impartial drawing of names of "sober, intelligent, and judicious" persons to serve as jurors in the various county courts.

Poor Directors.—In some counties the county commissioners serve as overseers of the poor, while in others they are elected the same as the other county officers. Their duties are the same in either case. They have general oversight of the county poorhouse and farm, paying out money from the county poor funds for the support and care of the poor or afflicted who need the assistance of their fellow-men during old age. The pay for these services varies in different sections; by general law they receive $3.50 a day and actual traveling expenses for their services in either capacity.

The County Superintendent of Schools is the highest school officer in the county. He is elected for three years by the school directors of the county in convention assembled. The county superintendent is to be a person (male or female), of good moral character, of literary and scientific acquirements, and skilled in the art of teaching. This official is only in a limited sense a county officer, being commissioned by the State superintendent of schools, and paid out of State funds. The salary is $4.50 for each school under his jurisdiction, except that it shall not be below a certain sum ($800), or over $2,000. The convention of school directors, however, may raise his salary, the additional amount to be paid out of the funds of the districts. The duties of the county superintendent of schools are to visit schools as often as practicable, to examine teachers, and issue certificates to such as are found to have the necessary qualifications, to conduct the annual county teachers' institute, as required by law, and to make report to the State superintendent as often as is required by law.

PART IV.

THE STATE.

CHAPTER XIX.

HISTORICAL.

In 1215 King John was forced to sign a document, enumerating certain rights, privileges, and immunities, which were to belong thereafter to all Englishmen. This was the famous Magna Charta. In 1628 the House of Commons forced King Charles I. to sign the "Petition of Right," defining more clearly and extending these rights. In 1679 the *habeas corpus* act was added to these others, making it impossible to keep a citizen in prison without trial, for an indefinite time. In 1689 Parliament forced the Stewart Kings to sign the Bill of Rights, which, with the preceding documents, was to form the bulwark of English liberty for succeeding generations. These rights, wrung from the heriditary rulers of England, during the preceding centuries, are all incorporated in the constitutions which form the basis or groundwork of all American governmental institutions. These constitutions refer to the people as the source of all authority.

"*A State* is a political community of free citizens,

occupying definite territory, organized under a government sanctioned and limited by a written constitution, and established by the consent of the people governed."—*Thorpe.*

CHAPTER XX.

THE LEGISLATURE.

THE LEGISLATIVE DEPARTMENT consists of two bodies called the House of Representatives, or Assembly, and the Senate. They make laws in harmony with the State and national Constitutions, and by authority of the people of the State. The State is divided into representative and senatorial districts. The representative districts are smaller than the senatorial, hence the membership of the House of Representatives is greater than that of the Senate. The lower House represents more nearly the local interests of the people. The number of members varies in different States. In Pennsylvania there are 204 representatives and 50 senators. The usual term of representatives is two years and senators four years. In many States they meet every two years, but are subject to the call of the Governor in extra session. The pay varies from $1.00 to $8.00 a day. In Pennsylvania the salary is $1,500 per session, with mileage, and a certain fixed sum for stationery and postage. The elections are held in November, and all the electors of the district have a voice in choosing these, their representatives. Their qualifications are fixed by the Constitution of the State.

CHAPTER XXI.

Executive Officers.

The Executive Department consists of the Governor and his secretaries, usually appointed.

The Governor is elected by the people at general election, in November, for a term of from one to four years. In Pennsylvania the term is four years, beginning on the third Tuesday of January next succeeding the election. The Governor is ineligible for re-election to succeed himself. The duties are, to see that the laws of the State are faithfully executed; he acts as commander of militia, appoints all officers not elected by the people (which appointments must be confirmed by the Senate), he fills vacancies, commissions his appointed officers, signs or vetoes bills passed by the legislature. He can pardon or reprieve criminals. In Pennsylvania a board of pardons must recommend a case to the Governor before he may take such action thereon. His salary is $10,000 a year.

The Lieutenant-Governor is elected at the same time and for the same term as the Governor. He presides over the Senate, and acts as Governor in case of vacancy in that office. Salary, $3,000 a year.

THE STATE. 45

The State Treasurer is chosen by the people at the general election, every second year, and is commissioned by the Governor to serve for two years from the first Monday of May next succeeding his election. His duties are to receive and receipt for all moneys paid into the State treasury, to pay all warrants drawn by the proper officers upon appropriations made by law. His salary is $5,000 a year.

The Auditor General is chosen by the people, at the general election, every third year, and serves for three years from the first Tuesday of May next succeeding his election. The duties of the auditor general are generally to examine and settle all accounts between the Commonwealth and any person, officer, department, association, or corporation. He examines annually and reports upon the condition of the State treasury. His salary is $3,000 a year.

The Secretary of Internal Affairs is chosen by the people at the general election every fourth year, and commissioned by the Governor to serve for four years from the first Tuesday of May following his election. It is his especial duty to exercise a watchful supervision over the railroad, banking, mining, manufacturing, and other business corporations of the State, and see that they confine themselves strictly within their corporate limits. He is a member of the board of pardons. His salary is $3,000 a year.

CHAPTER XXII.

Executive Officers (Continued).

The following are the more important of the State officers appointed by the Governor:

The Secretary of the Commonwealth is the head of the State department. He is appointed by the Governor and confirmed by the Senate. He is a member of the board of pardons. His duties bring him into intimate relations with the Governor, as nearly all the official transactions of the latter pass through his hands, and a record of all his official acts is kept in the State department. The secretary is the keeper of the seals of the State, and affixes them to, and countersigns such instruments as the law requires. He is paid $4,000 a year.

The Attorney General is appointed by the Governor at his pleasure, with the consent of the Senate. He is the legal adviser of the Governor and heads of departments. Salary $3,500 a year.

The Superintendent of Public Instruction is appointed by the Governor, with the advice and consent of the Senate, for the term of four years. He has general supervision of the schools of the Commonwealth, commissions county, city, and borough superintendents of the common schools, appoints and commissions trustees on the part of the State for State normal schools, conducts the annual examinations of students for graduation in the State normal schools, and appoints the State board of examiners. Whenever required he gives advice, explanations, construction, or information to the district officers, and to citizens, relative to the common school law, the duties of common school officers, the rights and duties of parents, guardians, pupils, and all others, the management of the schools, and all other questions and matters calculated to promote the cause of education, and signs all orders on the State treasurer for the payment of such moneys to the treasurers of the several school districts, as they may be entitled to receive from the State, and for all other moneys to be paid out of the appropriation to the common schools. His salary was fixed by the legislature of 1893 at $4,000 a year.

The Adjutant General is appointed by the Governor, with the consent of the Senate. He is chief of the Governor's staff, is his military executive officer, issues all orders to the national guard of the State, and is charged with their execution by the Governor.

The Insurance Commissioner is appointed by the Governor, with the advice and consent of the Senate, and commissioned to serve for three years from the first Monday of May next following his confirmation. His duties are to see that the insurance laws are faithfully executed. His salary is $3,000 a year.

Besides these officers mentioned there are various other boards and commissions which have charge of special work.

CHAPTER XXIII.

The State Judiciary.

The judicial power of the State is exercised by the Supreme Court, in some States called the Court of Appeals. Term of office, number of justices, compensation, etc., differ in different States. In Pennsylvania this court consists of seven justices, elected by the electors of the State at large: they hold office for twenty-one years, unless disqualified by misdemeanors; they are not eligible for re-election. The justice whose commission expires first is Chief Justice.

The jurisdiction of this court extends over the State. These justices may preside over Courts of Oyer and Terminer in the various counties, and have original jurisdiction in certain kinds of cases.

Appeals from the lower courts are carried to the Supreme Court, whose decisions are final, except in such cases as are designated in the Federal Constitution, which may be appealed to the United States Supreme Court.

The State is divided for convenience into three districts: the eastern, for which court sits at Philadelphia; the middle, for which court sits at Harrisburg; and the western, for which court sits at Pittsburg.

The salary of the Chief Justice is $8,500 a year; that of each justice of the Supreme Court is $8,000 a year.

In one sense all the lower courts are State courts, the judges being commissioned by the Governor, and paid from the State treasury, but they are here treated as belonging more especially to the limited territorial areas which elect them.

At present (January 1894) the Supreme Court consists of the following justices: Chief Justice—Hon. James P. Sterrett, Pittsburg; Justices—Hon. Henry Green, Easton, Northampton County; Hon. Henry W. Williams, Wellsboro, Tioga County; Hon. J. Brewster McCollum, Montrose, Susquehanna County; Hon. James T. Mitchell, Philadelphia; Hon. John Dean, of Hollidaysburg, Blair County; Hon. D. Newlin Fell, of Philadelphia.

PART V.

THE NATION.

CHAPTER XXIV.

HISTORICAL.

Besides the State governments, there is another, to which all the people of all the States are subject. This is called the United States government, and in certain matters it has authority over State governments. The people of all the States adopted another constitution. This United States Constitution establishes a superior government for all the people, called the national government.

History tells how thirteen British colonies, after seven long years of war, became thirteen sovereign States. How for mutual help and protection a confederation was formed which went into effect in 1781. It also tells that the plan of union thus outlined was soon found to be defective and imperfect. In this plan it was found that Congress had no power, except to recommend to the States things that should be done. Under menace of actual war, the States (or colonies) followed these recommendations, but as soon as peace was established the inherent weakness of the union began to manifest itself.

Some legislatures refused to raise money, some levied high duties, some low, and innumerable jealousies arose, which threatened the fair fabric which our forefathers had formed in war, and cemented with their best blood. So, in 1787, Congress passed a resolution providing for a convention of delegates from all the States. All except Rhode Island sent delegates as requested, and that body of statesmen formulated our present national Constitution, which has stood the test of more than a century of unprecedented growth and prosperity. The result in every emergency has proved the wisdom and far-seeing statesmanship of those noble men, who put aside all petty jealousies and local interests, and labored in the interest of posterity. It is one of the grandest documents ever made by man.

The government of the Confederation was a league, a federal government. That established by the Constitution is a national government with some federal features. This federal idea was allowed to remain, giving as much independence to the States as is consistent or compatible with strength in the central government.

The essential difference between the Articles of Confederation and the Constitution is seen in the first sentence of each. The former says, "The said States hereby severally enter into a firm league," etc., while the latter says, "We, the people of the United States, in order to form a more perfect union," etc., making the government depend upon the people themselves for its stability and permanence. The Civil War finally settled this question, establishing beyond a doubt the fact that the people of the whole Union constitute the nation.

The Constitution establishes legislative, executive, and judicial departments, and this was the model for nearly all the State Constitutions in this particular.

CHAPTER XXV.

Legislative Department.

CONGRESS.—This is the name given to the national legislative body. It is divided into a House of Representatives and a Senate. The members of the former body are elected by the people of the States every second year; those of the latter are elected by the State legislatures, and represent the States; and here we find a trace of the idea of the importance of the State, "State sovereignty."

The number of representatives is limited by the Constitution to one for every 30,000 inhabitants; but Congress increases the ratio of representation from time to time, to keep the House from becoming too large for comfort and control by the speaker; the ratio for the last census (1890) was one representative for every 173,901 inhabitants. Every State is entitled to at least one representative, even if its population falls below the constitutional limit of 30,000 inhabitants; the Constitution provides for this.

The Senate consists of two senators from each State; thus the House represents the people in general, the Senate, the States; the representation of all the States in the Senate is equal, each having the same number—two—no matter how large or how small. Texas and Rhode Island have equal representation. The members of the House represent the people who elect them, not by States, but in proportion to the population. The State legislature divides the State into Congressional districts.

A representative must be twenty-five years old, must have been a citizen for seven years, and must live in the State which elects him, though not in the district he represents. A senator must be thirty years of age, must have been a citizen for nine years, and must live in the State which he represents. Representatives are chosen for two years; senators for six.

The House chooses all its own officers, and has the sole right of impeachment. The Vice-President of the United States is the Chairman of the Senate, and can only vote when his vote will "break a tie." The Senate acts as court of judgment in all cases of impeachment.

CHAPTER XXVI.

LEGISLATIVE DEPARTMENT (Continued.)

Congress meets every year in December, but "A Congress" consists of the first two sessions of Congress following an election. Each House has its own general rules, appoints its own committees, and does its work independently, having no connection with the other House.

A committee is a subordinate body appointed by the chairman of either House, consisting of selected members from the body. The duty of these bodies is to consider certain matters previous to the action of the House to which they belong. Their actions are subject to the will of their House in all cases. A bill may originate in either House, and after passing that House must go to the other. Then it passes to the President, who either signs or vetoes it. But revenue bills must originate in the lower House, and the Senate may amend them as well as others. A vetoed bill may be passed "over the President's veto" by a second vote of both Houses, if there is a two thirds majority in favor of passing the bill.

The special powers, privileges, and restrictions of Congress are enumerated in the Constitution, and all powers not here delegated to the United States government are considered by the Tenth Amendment to the Constitution as being reserved to the several States, or to the people.

The salaries of representatives and senators are fixed by Congress itself, and are paid out of the national treasury. That of a member of the lower House is $5,000; that of a senator is the same. The The Speaker of the lower House gets $8,000; the

Vice-President, or Speaker of the Senate, also gets $8,000. The number of representatives from the State of Pennsylvania is at present (1893) 30; the whole number in the House of Representatives being 356 (1890 to 1900). The whole number of senators at present is 88.

CHAPTER XXVII.

EXECUTIVE DEPARTMENT.

This department of the government applies the laws after they have been made by the legislative and interpreted by the judicial departments. It is vested in a President or chief executive, and a cabinet composed of the heads of certain departments and commissions established by Congress at different times to assist the President in performing the duties devolved upon him as head of this department in the government of the nation.

The President must be a native-born citizen of the United States, and must have attained the age of thirty-five years, besides having the ordinary qualifications of an elector.

A President is elected every four years by a body of presidential electors who are chosen by the people on the first Tuesday after the first Monday in November. This body of electors constitutes what is called the Electoral College. It is composed of as many delegates from each State as that State has senators and representatives in Congress. These electors meet on the second Monday of January, usually in their respective State capitals, and vote by ballot for President and Vice-President. Three lists are then made which are called "returns." These are signed and certified and two of them transmitted sealed to the President of the Senate at Washington, and one is left with the judges of the United States District Court where the electors met. These lists are opened in the presence of the Senate and House of Representatives, and the votes counted on the second Wednesday of February. The ones who receive the greatest number of votes are declared to be elected, provided the number of votes received be a majority of all the electors appointed. If no person receive such a majority then the election of President falls upon the House of Representatives, and that of Vice-President devolves upon the Senate.

The President sees that the laws are properly executed, acts as commander-in-chief of the army and navy of the nation, and the militia of the several States when in the service of the United States; makes treaties, and appoints ambassadors, consuls, foreign ministers, judges of the Supreme Court, cabinet officers, and other inferior officers, as postmasters, etc., with the consent of two thirds of the Senate; sends messages to Congress; convenes extra sessions of Congress, and receives foreign ministers. His salary is $50,000 a year.

CHAPTER XXVIII.

EXECUTIVE DEPARTMENT (Continued).

The Vice-President must have the same qualifications as the President. He is the presiding officer of the Senate; he becomes President if, on account of death, resignation, or other constitutional disability of the President, the executive chair becomes vacant. It will be seen that the Vice-President is not a regular executive officer unless he becomes President; his duties as chairman of the Senate are of a legislative character. His salary is $8,000 a year.

THE CABINET OFFICERS are: Secretary of state, secretary of war, secretary of the treasury, secretary of the navy, secretary of interior, secretary of agriculture, postmaster general, and attorney general. These officers are at the head of their respective departments, and they have charge of all matters relating to them. They meet regularly with the President and discuss national affairs, and constitute a board of political advisers. The salary of each is $8,000 a year.

The Secretary of State is the only officer in our federal government who has the power to communicate with other governments in the name of the President. He negotiates treaties, and has charge of the great seal of the United States.

The Secretary of the Treasury has charge of the finances of the nation, coining money and issuing treasury notes. He can be called upon to suggest means of maintaining national credit or creating revenues. His most important duty is the management of the debt.

The Secretary of War has charge of the military affairs of the nation. He keeps the records of the army, and takes measures for the survey of the harbors and improvement of navigation. He also has charge of the signal service and weather bureau.

The Secretary of the Navy, under the direction of the President, manages the naval affairs of the nation. The naval observatory at Washington is under the charge of this department.

The Secretary of the Interior is intrusted with the management of matters relative to public land, Indians, schools, pensions, and patents. He has charge of the census, and manages home or domestic affairs generally.

The Postmaster General has the charge of the postal interests of the nation. He appoints postmasters whose salaries are below $1,000, and controls the style of stamps and postal cards.

The Attorney General is the chief law officer of the nation. He represents the United States in all suits at law in which the United States is a party.

The Secretary of Agriculture is intrusted with the agricultural interests of the country. He manages all agricultural experiment stations, and issues crop statistics.

Under these heads of departments are various

commissions and bureaus, having special work to do. This subdivision simplifies the work and makes it more effective.

CHAPTER XXIX.

JUDICIAL DEPARTMENT.

The Constitution provides for a national judicial department, consisting of a Supreme Court, with inferior courts, established from time to time. These inferior courts are of two kinds : circuit courts, nine in number, and district courts, at present (1894) sixty-four in number.

The Supreme Court consists of a Chief Justice and eight associatiate justices appointed by the President to hold office for life, unless removed by impeachment. This court holds one session each year, lasting from October until May. It hears cases appealed from the lower courts, and has original jurisdiction in cases affecting foreign ministers and consuls, and those in which a State is a party. The salary of Chief Justice is $10,500 a year; that of associate justice, $10,000 a year.

The circuit courts, nine in number, are presided over by circuit judges appointed by the President for life, unless removed by impeachment. Each one of the nine supreme justices must visit a circuit and hold court at least once in two years. Besides these, two regular circuit courts are held annually, presided over by the circuit judge, alone or with the district judge of the district in which court is sitting, There are circuit court commissioners, appointed by the judge of the circuit, who help in the arrest, examination, and committal of persons accused of offenses against the national government. These commissioners are the most numerous and widely distributed of federal judicial officers. As a State judicial officer or justice of the peace acts in State matters, so a circuit commissioner acts in matters of federal offense. But as these commissioners are not always on hand, any judge or magistrate, of either the State or federal government, is empowered to act as a commissioner. He has no legal right to act in federal matters if he be a State officer, but if necessity arise, he may become a national officer, and act as such.

In 1891 Congress established in each circuit a court of appeals, consisting of three judges, who hear appeals from the circuit court. Circuit courts hear appeals from the district courts. The district and circuit courts may have original jurisdiction in a great variety of cases involving offenses against the United States.

The district courts, sixty-four in number at present, are the lowest federal courts. Every State has at least one judicial district, and some have two; New York, Texas, and Alabama have three each. In a few cases one judge supplies two or more districts. There are in most districts four terms held annually, and some special terms. The district judge is appointed by the President, for the same time as in the higher federal courts. There is a federal district attorney in most districts, appointed by the President, whose duty it is to prosecute criminal cases, and to appear in all civil cases before the resident district judge who presides over the district court; he also appoints a United States marshal, whose duties are those of a sheriff of the district, in all federal cases. District court may try any cases committed against the United States in the district, except such as are punishable by death. The resident district judge has an annual salary of $5,000.

The United States Court of Claims is a court established by Congress for the settlement of certain claims which otherwise would have to be settled by Congress. In this court only can suit be brought against the government. If the suit is decided in favor of the claimant, the case is referred to Congress, whose business it is to see that the claim is settled.

CHAPTER XXX.

THE NATION.*

The nation is the people, not as a confederation of individuals, but as a moral unit. It is distinct from a party or a faction. It is distinct from the offices

---
*Most of this chapter is abridged from Thorpe's delightful work on Civil Government.

created in its formal expression of government. It is distinct from its constitution and its treaties. Its elements are the people and the land. Natural boundaries alone can determine its confines. The waves of the sea, the cold of the North, the heat of the South, will ultimately divide us from the lands of other nations.

The nation alone is sovereign. Its will is expressed from time to time by its chosen representatives acting together in convention. The nation is older than the written constitution. As a sovereign it determines for itself its aim and its object in history. It declares its will and embodies its spirit in its institutions. The government of the people of the United States is the formal expression of the will of the nation. The unwritten constitution is the development of the nation in history, its customs, its laws, its opinions, its moral sense finding expression in its institutions. The written constitution is changed by the will of the people. Social revolutions, industrial changes, political revolutions, cause changes in the written supreme law of the land. At critical times in the nation's history the constitution is naught, and the people by their decision impart a new meaning to the formal instrument. The existence of it is necessary to the existence of the nation, and the nation to the existence of the citizen. The nation is not apart from the citizen; he is in and of the nation. In it and through it he realizes his rights and is protected in them. The citizen has his own destiny to work out consistent with the moral order of the world. All he realizes is made possible to him by his own nature, and he is responsible for the exercise of his own powers. When every citizen is conscious of his industrial, his political, his social, and his moral nature, then, has the nation its full strength and the citizen a realization of a complete life. The nation complements the activities of the citizen and institutes and maintains for his benefit a field for his reasonable and normal development. The nation is thus bound to educate the citizen harmoniously, offering him opportunities for industrial, political, social, and moral training. Its constant function is to place within his reach the realization of his loftiest hopes and purposes, and to exalt his manhood and ennoble human life with human sympathy. The majesty of law, the authority of government, the solemn declaration of treaties and constitutions gather like a benediction on the sacredness of the family and the home.

The foes of the nation are the forces that would disintegrate it and with which it wages a perpetual conflict. Communism seeks social perfection in a common interest in all property, persons, and things ; it destroys the family and private property, it attacks the foundations of modern society. Socialism seeks to wipe out all laws, manners, customs, the guarantees of property and person, and to reorganize society on a different basis. The reforms suggested have been dictated by every fancy, and have been usually absurd and destructive of all civil government. Nihilism is a negation of all government. It seeks to overthrow all existing forms, by assassination, dynamite, and the like revolutionary measures. Anarchism, like nihilism, is a form of lawlessness that would overturn all the laws of organized society, destroy the home, the church, the school,—everything that is dear to liberty-loving and industrious people. Societies and individuals, holding and teaching these destructive ideas, have caused riot and bloodshed in our own country.

We harbor foreigners who hold these ideas which are at war with those that lie at the very foundation of our free government. It is the duty of the American citizen to know his rights and to perform his duty; to eradicate by lawful means all influences injurious to the peace and welfare of his native land.

Centuries pass; new faces come and go; new voices are heard over the earth; other hands labor, and other men enter into their labors with the glory of new duties and the enthusiasm of the exercise of new rights. A pure morality, a lofty statesmanship, devotion among the people to the rights and duties of citizenship, alone keep the nation from decay. Invention and discovery ameliorate the condition of men. Science and art enlarge the bounds of human knowledge, but the nation alone can carry on the work of history. Our flag is the symbol of the nation. To an American it is an object of veneration, to the people of other lands it is the symbol of liberty, union, peace, happiness, and prosperity. Wherever the flag floats the voice of the nation is heard. The honor of the nation is the honor of its flag. To the people of the United States are intrusted sacred interests. Every citizen is the keeper in trust of the happiness of himself and those who will come after him. This people is to work out the realization of human rights, industrially, politically, socially, and morally. It is for us to realize the hopes of humanity, to be the answer to the prayers of the ages.

Popular government is the great experiment of history. We cannot turn back. We are one of an argosy of nations moving onward, toward the freedom of humanity.

DECLARATION OF INDEPENDENCE.

IN CONGRESS, JULY 4, 1776.

The Unanimous Declaration of the Thirteen United States of America.

When, in the course of human events, it becomes necessary for one people to dissolve the political bands which have connected them with one another, and to assume, among the powers of the earth, the separate and equal station to which the laws of nature and of nature's God entitle them, a decent respect to the opinions of mankind requires that they should declare the causes which impel them to the separation.

We hold these truths to be self-evident, that all men are created equal; that they are endowed by their Creator with certain unalienable rights; that among these are life, liberty and the pursuit of happiness. That, to secure these rights, governments are instituted among men, deriving their just powers from the consent of the governed; that whenever any form of government becomes destructive of these ends, it is the right of the people to alter or abolish it, and to institute a new government, laying its foundations on such principles, and organizing its powers in such form, as to them shall seem most likely to effect their safety and happiness. Prudence, indeed, will dictate that governments long established should not be changed for light and transient causes; and accordingly, all experience hath shown, that mankind are more disposed to suffer, while evils are sufferable, than to right themselves by abolishing the forms to which they are accustomed. But, when a long train of abuses and usurpations, pursuing invariably the same object, evinces a design to reduce them under absolute despotism, it is their right, it is their duty, to throw off such government, and to provide new guards for their future security. Such has been the patient sufferance of these colonies, and such is now the necessity which constrains them to alter their former systems of government. The history of the present king of Great Britain is a history of repeated injuries and usurpations, all having, in direct object, the establishment of an absolute tyranny over these States. To prove this, let facts be submitted to a candid world:

He has refused his assent to laws the most wholesome and necessary for the public good.

He has forbidden his governors to pass laws of immediate and pressing importance, unless suspended in their operations till his assent should be obtained; and when so suspended, he has utterly neglected to attend to them.

He has refused to pass other laws for the accommodation of large districts of people, unless those people would relinquish the right of representation in the legislature; a right inestimable to them, and formidable to tyrants only.

He has called together legislative bodies at places unusual, uncomfortable, and distant from the repository of their public records, for the sole purpose of fatiguing them into compliance with his measures.

He has dissolved representative houses repeatedly,

for opposing, with manly firmness, his invasions on the rights of the people.

He has refused, for a long time after such dissolutions, to cause others to be elected; whereby the legislative powers, incapable of annihilation, have returned to the people at large for their exercise; the State remaining, in the meantime, exposed to all the dangers of invasions from without, and convulsions within.

He has endeavored to prevent the population of these States; for that purpose, obstructing the laws for the naturalization of foreigners, refusing to pass others to encourage their migration hither, and raising the conditions of new appropriations of lands.

He has obstructed the administration of justice, by refusing his assent to laws for establishing judiciary powers.

He has made judges dependent on his will alone for the tenure of their offices and the amount and payment of their salaries.

He has erected a multitude of new offices, and sent hither swarms of officers to harass our people and eat their substance.

He has kept among us, in times of peace, standing armies, without the consent of our legislatures.

He has affected to render the military independent of, and superior to, the civil power.

He has combined, with others, to subject us to a jurisdiction foreign to our constitutions, and unacknowledged by our laws; giving his assent to their acts of pretended legislation:

For quartering large bodies of armed troops among us:

For protecting them, by a mock trial, from punishment, for any murders which they should commit on the inhabitants of these States:

For cutting off our trade with all parts of the world:

For imposing taxes on us without our consent:

For depriving us, in many cases, of the benefit of trial by jury:

For transporting us beyond seas to be tried for pretended offenses:

For abolishing the free system of English laws in a neighboring province, establishing therein an arbitrary government, and enlarging its boundries, so as to render it at once an example and fit instrument for introducing the same absolute rule into these colonies:

For taking away our charters, abolishing our most valuable laws, and altering, fundamentally, the forms of our governments:

For suspending our own legislatures, and declaring themselves invested with power to legislate for us in all cases whatsoever:

He has abdicated government here, by declaring us out of his protection, and waging war against us.

He has plundered our seas, ravaged our coasts, burned our towns, and destroyed the lives of our people.

He is, at this time, transporting large armies of foreign mercenaries to complete the works of death, desolation, and tyranny already begun, with circumstances of cruelty and perfidy scarcely paralleled in the most barbarous ages, and totally unworthy the head of a civilized nation.

He has constrained our fellow-citizens, taken captive on the high seas, to bear arms against their country, to become the executioners of their friends and brethren, or to fall themselves by their hands.

He has excited domestic insurrection among us, and has endeavored to bring on the inhabitants of our frontiers, the merciless Indian savages, whose known rule of warfare is an undistinguished destruction of all ages, sexes, and conditions.

In every stage of these oppressions, we have petitioned for redress, in the most humble terms; our repeated petitions have been answered only by repeated injury. A prince, whose character is thus marked by every act which may define a tyrant, is unfit to be the ruler of a free people.

Nor have we been wanting in our attentions to our British brethren. We have warned them, from time to time, of attempts by their legislature to extend an unwarrantable jurisdiction over us. We have reminded them of the circumstances of our emigration and settlement here. We have appealed to their native justice and magnanimity, and we have conjured them, by the ties of our common kindred, to disavow these usurpations, which would inevitably interrupt our connections and correspondence. They, too, have been deaf to the voice of justice and of consanguinity. We must, therefore, acquiesce in the necessity, which denounces our separation, and hold them, as we hold the rest of mankind, enemies in war, in peace, friends.

We, therefore, the representatives of the UNITED STATES OF AMERICA, IN GENERAL CONGRESS assembled, appealing to the Supreme Judge of the World for the rectitude of our intentions, do, in the name, and by the authority of the good people of these colonies, solemnly publish and declare, That these United Colonies are, and of right ought to be, FREE AND INDEPENDENT STATES; that they are absolved from all allegiance to the British crown, and that all political connection between them and the State of Great Britain, is, and ought to be, totally dissolved; and that as *FREE AND INDEPEND-*

ENT STATES, they have full power to levy war, conclude peace, contract alliances, establish commerce, and do all other acts and things which INDEPENDENT STATES may of right do. And, for the support of this declaration, with a firm reliance on the protection of DIVINE PROVIDENCE, we mutually pledge to each other, our lives, our fortunes, and our sacred honor.

SIGNERS :

New Hampshire.
Josiah Bartlett.
William Whipple.
Matthew Thornton.

Massachusetts.
John Hancock.
John Adams.
Samuel Adams.
Robert Treat Paine.
Elbridge Gerry.

Rhode Island.
Stephen Hopkins.
William Ellery.

Connecticut.
Roger Sherman.
Samuel Huntington.
William Williams.
Oliver Wolcott.

New York.
William Floyd.
Philip Livingston.
Francis Lewis.
Lewis Morris.

New Jersey.
Richard Stockton.
John Witherspoon.
Francis Hopkinson.
John Hart.
Abraham Clark.

Pennsylvania.
Robert Morris.
Benjamin Rush.
Benjamin Franklin.
John Morton.
George Clymer.

James Smith.
George Taylor.
James Wilson.
George Ross.

Delaware.
Cæsar Rodney.
George Read.
Thomas McKean.

Maryland.
Samuel Chase.
Thomas Stone.
William Paca.
Charles Carroll, of Carrollton.

Virginia.
George Wythe.
Richard Henry Lee.
Thomas Jefferson.
Benjamin Harrison.
Thomas Nelson, Jr.
Francis Lightfoot Lee.
Carter Braxton.

North Carolina.
William Hooper.
Joseph Hewes.
John Penn.

South Carolina.
Edward Rutledge.
Thomas Heyward, Jr.
Thomas Lynch, Jr.
Arthur Middleton.

Georgia.
Button Gwinnett.
Lyman Hall.
George Walton.

ARTICLES OF CONFEDERATION.

Articles of Confederation and Perpetual Union between the States of New Hampshire, Massachusetts Bay, Rhode Island and Providence Plantations, Connecticut, New York, New Jersey, Pennsylvania, Delaware, Maryland, Virginia, North Carolina, South Carolina, and Georgia :

ARTICLE I.—The style of this confederacy shall be, "The United States of America."

ART. II.—Each State retains its sovereignty, freedom, and independence, and every power, jurisdiction, and right, which is not by this confederation expressly delegated to the United States in Congress assembled.

ART. III.—The said States hereby severally enter into a firm league of friendship with each other, for their common defense, the securitiy of their liberties, and their mutual and general welfare, binding themselves to assist each other against all force offered to, or attacks made upon them, or any of them, on account of religion, sovereignty, trade, or any other pretense whatever.

ART. IV.—The better to secure and perpetuate mutual friendship and intercourse among the people of the different States in this Union, the free inhabitants of each of these States, paupers, vagabonds, and fugitives from justice excepted, shall be entitled to all privileges and immunities of free citizens in the several States, and the people of each State shall have free ingress and egress to and from any other State, and shall enjoy therein all the privileges of trade and commerce, subject to the same duties, impositions, and restrictions, as the inhabitants thereof respectively: *Provided*, That such restrictions shall not extend so far as to prevent the removal of property imported into any State to any other State of which the owner is an inhabitant: *Provided, also*, That no imposition, duties, or restrictions shall be laid by any State on the property of the United States or either of them.

If any person guilty of, or charged with, treason, felony, or other high misdemeanor in any State, shall flee from justice, and be found in any of the United States, he shall, upon demand of the governor, or executive power of the State from which he fled, be delivered up, and removed to the State having jurisdiction of his offense. Full faith and credit shall be given, in each of these States, to the records, acts, and judicial proceedings of the courts and magistrates of every other State.

ART. V.—For the more convenient management of the general interests of the United States, delegates shall be annually appointed, in such manner as the legislature of each State shall direct, to meet in Congress on the first Monday in November, in every year, with a power reserved to each State to recall its delegates, or any of them, at any time within the year, and to send others in their stead for the remainder of the year.

No State shall be represented in Congress by less than two, nor by more than seven members ; and no person shall be capable of being a delegate for more than three years in any term of six years ; nor shall any person, being a delegate, be capable of holding any office under the United States for which he, or another for his benefit, receives any salary, fees, or emolument of any kind.

Each State shall maintain its own delegates in any meeting of the States and while they act as members of the committee of the States.

In determining questions in the United States in Congress assembled, each State shall have one vote.

Freedom of speech and debate in Congress shall not be impeached or questioned in any court or place out of Congress; and the members of Congress shall be protected in their persons from arrests and imprisonments during the time of their going to and from, and attendance on Congress, except for treason, felony, or breach of peace.

ART. VI.—No State, without the consent of the United States, in Congress assembled, shall send any embassy to, or receive any embassy from, or enter into any conference, agreement, alliance, or treaty, with any king, prince, or State; nor shall any person holding any office of profit or trust under the United States, or any of them, accept of any present, emolument, office, or title of any kind whatever, from any king, prince, or foreign State; nor shall the United States, in Congress assembled, or any of them, grant any title of nobility.

No two or more States shall enter into any treaty, confederation, or alliance whatever between them, without the consent of the United States, in Congress assembled, specifying accurately the purpose for which the same is to be entered into, and how long it shall continue.

No State shall lay any imposts or duties which may interfere with any stipulations in treaties entered into by the United States, in Congress assembled, with any king, prince, or State, in pursuance of any treaties already proposed by Congress to the courts of France and Spain.

No vessels of war shall be kept up in time of peace,

by any State, except such number only as, in the judgment of the United States, in Congress assembled, shall be deemed requisite to garrison the forts necessary for the defense of such State: but every State shall always keep up a well-regulated and disciplined militia, sufficiently armed and accoutered, and shall provide and constantly have ready for use, in public stores, a due number of field-pieces and tents, and a proper quantity of arms, ammunition, and camp equipage.

No State shall engage in any war without the consent of the United States, in Congress assembled, unless such State is actually invaded by enemies, or shall have received certain advice of a resolution being formed by some nation of Indians to invade such State, and the danger is so immediate as not to admit of a delay till the United States, in Congress assembled, can be consulted; nor shall any State grant commissions to any ships or vessels of war, nor letters of marque or reprisal except it be after a declaration of war by the United States, in Congress assembled, and then only against the kingdom or state, and the subjects thereof against which war has been so declared, and under such regulations as shall be established by the United States, in Congress assembled, unless such State be infested by pirates, in which case vessels of war may be fitted out for that occasion, and kept so long as the danger shall continue, or until the United States, in Congress assembled, shall determine otherwise.

ART. VII.—When land forces are raised by any State for the common defense, all officers of or under rank of colonel, shall be appointed by the legislature of each State respectively by whom such forces shall be raised, or in such manner as such State shall direct, and all vacancies shall be filled up by the State which first made the appointment.

ART. VIII.—All charges of war, and all other expenses that shall be incurred for the common defense or general welfare, and allowed by the United States, in Congress assembled, shall be defrayed out of a common treasury, which shall be supplied by the several States, in proportion to the value of all land within each State, granted to, or surveyed for, any person, as such land and the buildings and improvements thereon shall be estimated according to such mode as the United States, in Congress assembled, shall, from time to time, direct and appoint. The taxes for paying that proportion shall be laid and levied by the authority and direction of the legislatures of the several States, within the time agreed upon by the United States in Congress assembled.

ART. IX.—The United States, in Congress assembled, shall have the sole and exclusive right and power of determining on peace and war except in the cases mentioned in the sixth Article; of sending and receiving ambassadors; entering into treaties and alliances, provided that no treaty of commerce shall be made whereby the legislative power of the respective States shall be restrained from imposing such imposts and duties on foreigners as their own people are subjected to, or from prohibiting the exportation or importation of any species of goods or commodities whatsoever; of establishing rules for deciding, in all cases, what captures on land or water shall be legal, and in what manner prizes taken by land or naval forces in the service of the United States shall be divided or appropriated; of granting letters of marque and reprisal in times of peace; appointing courts for the trial of piracies and felonies committed on the high seas; and establishing courts for receiving and determining finally appeals in all cases of captures: *Provided*, That no member of Congress shall be appointed a judge of any of the said courts.

The United States, in Congress assembled, shall be the last resort on appeal in all disputes and differences subsisting, or that hereafter may arise between two or more States concerning boundary, jurisdiction, or any other cause whatever; which authority shall always be exercised in the manner following: Whenever the legislative or executive authority, or lawful agent of any State in controversy with another, shall present a petition to Congress stating the matter in question and praying for a hearing, notice thereof shall be given by order of Congress, to the legislative or executive authority of the other States in controversy, and a day assigned for the appearance of the parties by their lawful agents, who shall then be directed to appoint by joint consent, commissioners or judges to constitute a court for hearing and determining the matter in question; but if they can not agree, Congress shall name three persons, out of each of the United States, and from the list of such persons each party shall alternately strike out one, the petitioners beginning, until the numbers shall be reduced to thirteen; and from that number not less than seven nor more than nine names, as Congress shall direct, shall, in the presence of Congress, be drawn out by lot; and the persons whose names shall be so drawn, or any five of them, shall be commissioners or judges to hear and finally determine the controversy, so always as a major part of the judges who shall hear the cause shall agree in the determination; and if either party shall neglect to attend at the day appointed, without showing reasons which Congress shall judge sufficient, or, being present, shall refuse to strike, the

Congress shall proceed to nominate three persons out of each State, and the secretary of Congress shall strike in behalf of such party absent or refusing, and the judgment and sentence of the court, to be appointed in the manner before prescribed, shall be final and conclusive; and if any of the parties shall refuse to submit to the authority of such court, or to appear or defend their claim or cause, the court shall nevertheless proceed to pronounce sentence or judgment, which shall in like manner be final and decisive; the judgment or sentence and other proceedings being in either case transmitted to Congress, and lodged among the acts of Congress for the security of the parties concerned; provided that every commissioner, before he sits in judgment, shall take an oath, to be administered by one of the judges of the Supreme or Superior Court of the State where the cause shall be tried, "well and truly to hear and determine the matter in question, according to the best of his judgment, without favor, affection, or hope of reward:" *Provided*, *also*, That no State shall be deprived of territory for the benefit of the United States.

All controversies concerning the private right of soil claimed under different grants of two or more States, whose jurisdiction, as they may respect such lands, and the States which passed such grants are adjusted, the said grants or either of them being at the same time claimed to have originated antecedent to such settlement of jurisdiction, shall, on the petition of either party to Congress of the United States, be finally determined, as near as may be, in the same manner as is before prescribed for deciding disputes respecting territorial jurisdiction between different States.

The United States, in Congress assembled, shall

also have the sole and exclusive right and power of regulating the alloy and value of coin struck by their own authority or by that of the respective States; fixing the standard of weights and measures throughout the United States; regulating the trade and managing all affairs with Indians, not members of any of the States, provided that the legislative rights of any State, within its own limits, be not infringed or violated; establishing and regulating post-offices from one State to another throughout all the United States, and exacting such postage on the papers passing through the same, as may be requisite to defray the expense of the said office; appointing all officers of the land forces in the service of the United States, excepting regimental officers; appointing all the officers of the naval forces, and commissioning all officers whatever in the service of the United States; making rules for the government and regulation of the said land and naval forces, and directing their operations.

The United States, in Congress assembled, shall have authority to appoint a committee, to sit in the recess of Congress, to be denominated "A Committee of the States," and to consist of one delegate from each State: and to appoint such other committees and civil officers as may be necessary for managing the general affairs of the United States under their direction; to appoint one of their number to preside, provided that no person be allowed to serve in office of president more than one year in any term of three years; to ascertain the necessary sums of money to be raised for the service of the United States, and to appropriate and apply the same for defraying the public expenses; to borrow money or emit bills on the credit of the United States, transmitting every half year to the respective States an account of the sums of money so borrowed or emitted; to build and equip a navy; to agree upon the number of land forces, and to make requisitions from each State for its quota, in proportion to the number of white inhabitants in such State, which requisition shall be binding; and thereupon the legislature of each State shall appoint the regimental officers, raise the men, and clothe, arm, and equip them in a soldier-like manner at the expense of the United States; and the officers and men so clothed, armed, and equipped shall march to the place appointed, and within the time agreed on by the United States, in Congress assembled; but if the United States, in Congress assembled, shall, in consideration of circumstances, judge proper that any State should not raise men, or should raise a smaller number than its quota, and that any other State should raise a greater number of men than the quota thereof, such extra number shall be raised, officered, clothed, armed, and equipped in the same manner as the quota of such State, unless the legislature of such State shall judge that such extra number cannot be safely spared out of the same, in which case they shall raise, officer, clothe, arm, and equip as many of such extra number as they judge can be safely spared, and the officers and men so clothed, armed, and equipped shall march to the place appointed, and within the time agreed on by the United States, in Congress assembled.

The United States, in Congress assembled, shall never engage in a war nor grant letters of marque and reprisal in time of peace, nor enter into any treaties or alliances, nor coin money, nor regulate the value thereof, nor ascertain the sums and expenses necessary for the defense and welfare of the United States, or any of them, nor emit bills, nor borrow money on the credit of the United States, nor appropriate money, nor agree upon the number of vessels of war to be built or purchased, or the number of land or sea forces to be raised, nor appoint a commander-in-chief of the army or navy, unless nine States assent to the same, nor shall a question on any other point, except for adjourning from day to day, be determined, unless by the votes of a majority of the United States, in Congress assembled.

The Congress of the United States shall have power to adjourn to any time within the year, and to any place within the United States, so that no period of adjournment be for a longer duration than the space of six months, and shall publish the journal of their proceedings monthly, except such parts thereof relating to treaties, alliances or military operations as in their judgment require secrecy; and the yeas and nays of the delegates of each State, on any question, shall be entered on the journal, when it is desired by any delegate; and the delegates of a State, or any of them, at his or their request, shall be furnished with a transcript of the said journal, except such parts as are above excepted, to lay before the legislatures of the several States.

ART. X.—The committee of the States, or any nine of them, shall be authorized to execute, in the recess of Congress, such of the powers of Congress as the United States, in Congress assembled, by the consent of nine States, shall from time to time, think expedient to vest them with, provided that no power be delegated to the said committee, for the exercise of which, by the articles of the confederation, the voice of nine States, in the Congress of the United States assembled, is requisite.

ART. XI.—Canada acceding to this confederation

and joining in the measures of the United States, shall be admitted into, and entitled to all the advantages of this Union; but no other colony shall be admitted into the same unless such admission be agreed to by nine States.

ART. XII.—All bills of credit emitted, moneys borrowed and debts contracted by or under the authority of Congress, before the assembling of the United States, in pursuance of the present confederation, shall be deemed and considered as a charge against the United States, for payment and satisfaction whereof the said United States and the public faith are hereby solemnly pledged.

ART. XIII.—Every State shall abide by the determinations of the United States, in Congress assembled, on all questions which by this Confederation are submitted to them. And the Articles of this Confederation shall be inviolably observed by every State; and the Union shall be perpetual; nor shall any alteration at any time hereafter be made in any of them, unless such alteration be agreed to in a Congress of the United States; and be afterwards confirmed by the legislature of every State.

And whereas it hath pleased the great Governor of the world to incline the hearts of the legislatures we respectively represent in Congress, to approve of, and to authorize us to ratify the said Articles of Confederation and perpetual Union, know ye, that we, the undersigned delegates, by virtue of the power and authority to us given for that purpose, do, by these presents, in the name and in behalf of our respective constituents, fully and entirely ratify and confirm each and every one of the said Articles of Confederation and perpetual Union, and all and singular the matters and things therein contained: and we do further solemnly plight and engage the faith of our respective constituents, that they shall abide by the determinations of the United States, in Congress assembled, on all questions which by the said Confederation are submitted to them ; and that the articles thereof shall be inviolably observed by the States we respectively represent, and that the Union shall be perpetual.

In witness whereof we have hereunto set our hands in Congress. Done at Philadelphia, in the State of Pennsyvania, the ninth day of July, in the year of our Lord, 1778, and in the third year of the Independence of America.

PART OF THE ORDINANCE OF 1787.

JULY 13, 1787.

An Ordinance for the Government of the Territory of the United States Northwest of the River Ohio.

It is hereby ordained and declared, by the authority aforesaid, that the following Articles shall be considered as Articles of Compact between the original States and the people and States in the said Territory, and forever remain unalterable, unless by common consent, to-wit:

ARTICLE I.—No person demeaning himself in a peaceable and orderly manner, shall ever be molested on account of his mode of worship or religious sentiments in the said Territory.

ART. II.—The inhabitants of the said Territory shall always be entitled to the benefit of the writ of *habeas corpus*, and of trial by jury; of a proportionate representation of the people in the legislature, and of judicial proceedings according to the course of the common law. All persons shall be bailable unless for capital offenses, where the proof shall be evident or the presumption great. All fines shall be moderate, and no cruel or unusual punishments shall be inflicted. No man shall be deprived of his liberty or propery, but by the judgment of his peers, or the law of the land; and should the public exigencies make it necessary for the common preservation to take any person's property, or to demand his particular services, full compensation shall be made for the same, and in the just preservation of rights and property, it is understood and declared, that no law ought ever to be made, or have force in the said Territory, that shall in any manner whatever interfere with, or affect private contracts or engagements, *bona fide* and without fraud previously formed.

ART. III.—Religion, morality, and knowledge being necessary to good government and the happiness of mankind, schools, and the means of education, shall forever be encouraged. The utmost good faith shall always be observed toward the Indians; their lands and property shall never be taken from them without their consent; and in their property, rights, and liberty they shall never be invaded or disturbed, unless in just and lawful wars authorized by Congress; but laws founded in justice and humanity, shall, from time to time, be made, for preventing wrongs being done to them, and for preserving peace and friendship with them.

ART. IV.—The said Territory and the States which may be formed therein, shall forever remain a part of this confederacy of the United States of America, subject to the Articles of Confederation, and to such alteration therein, as shall be constitutionally made; and to all the acts and ordinances of the United States, in Congress assembled, conformable thereto. The inhabitants and settlers in the said Territory shall be subject to pay a part of the federal debts contracted, or to be contracted, and a proportional part of the expenses of government, to be apportioned on them, by Congress, according to the same common rule and measure by which apportionments thereof shall be made on the other States; and the taxes for paying their proportion shall be laid and levied by the authority and direction of the legislatures of the district or districts, or new States, as in the original States, within the time agreed upon by the United States, in Congress assembled. The legislatures of those districts or new States, shall never interfere with the primary disposal of the soil by the United States, in Congress assembled, nor with any regulations Congress may find necessary for securing the title in such soil to the *bona fide* purchasers. No tax shall be imposed on lands the property of the United States; and in no case shall non-residents be taxed higher than residents. The navigable waters leading into the Mississippi and St. Lawrence, and the carrying places between the same, shall be common highways, and forever free, as well as to the inhabitants of the said Territory, as to the citizens of the United States, and those of any other States that may be admitted into the confederacy, without any tax, impost, or duty therefor.

ART. V.—There shall be formed in the said Territory not less than three, nor more than five States; and the boundaries of the States, as soon as Virginia shall alter her act of session and consent to the same, shall become fixed and established as follows, to-wit: The western State in the said Territory shall be bounded by the Mississippi, the Ohio, and the Wabash rivers; a direct line drawn, from the Wabash and Post Vincents due north to the territorial line between the United States and Canada, and by the said territorial line to the Lake of the Woods and Mississippi. The middle State shall be bounded by the said direct line, the Wabash from Post Vincents to the Ohio, by the Ohio, by a direct line drawn due north from the mouth of the Great Miami to the said territorial line, and by said territorial line. The eastern State shall be bounded by the last mentioned direct line, the Ohio, Pennsylvania, and the said territorial line: *Provided, however*, and it is further understood and declared, that the boundaries of these three States shall be subject so far to be altered that if Congress shall hereafter find it expedient, they shall have authority to form one or two States in that part of the said territory which lies north of an east and west line drawn through the southerly bend or extreme of Lake Michigan. And whenever any of the said States shall have sixty thousand free inhabitants therein, such State shall be admitted by its delegates, into the Congress of the United States, on an equal footing with the original States, in all respects whatsoever; and shall be at liberty to form a permanent constitution and State government: *Provided*, the constitution and government so to be formed shall be republican, and in conformity to the principles contained in these articles; and, so far as it can be consistent with the general interest of the confederacy such admission shall be allowed at an earlier period, and when there may be a less number of free inhabitants in the State than sixty thousand.

ART. VI.—Their shall be neither slavery nor involuntary servitude in the said Territory, otherwise than in the punishment of crimes whereof the party shall have been duly convicted: *Provided, always*, That any person escaping into the same, from whom labor or service is lawfully claimed in any one of the original States, such fugitive may be lawfully reclaimed and conveyed to the person claiming his or her labor or service as aforesaid. Be it ordained, by the authority aforesaid, that the resolutions of the 23rd of April, 1784, relative to the subject of this ordinance, be, and the same are hereby repealed.

CONSTITUTION OF THE UNITED STATES.

[This Constitution went into operation on the first Wednesday in March, 1789. 5 Wheat., 420.]

We, the people of the United States, in order to form a more perfect union, establish justice, insure domestic tranquility, provide for the common defense, promote the general welfare, and secure the blessings of liberty to ourselves and our posterity, do ordain and establish this Constitution of United States of America.

ARTICLE I.

SECTION I. All legislative powers herein granted, shall be vested in a Congress of the United States, which shall consist of a Senate, and House of Representatives.

SEC. II. (Clause 1.) The House of Representatives shall be composed of members chosen every second year by the people of the several States, and the electors in each State shall have the qualifications requisite for electors of the most numerous branch of the State legislature.

(Clause 2.) No person shall be a representative who shall not have attained to the age of twenty-five years, and been seven years a citizen of the United States, and who shall not when elected, be an inhabitant of that State in which he shall be chosen.

(Clause 3.) Representatives and direct taxes shall be apportioned among the several States which may be included within this Union, according to their respective numbers, which shall be determined by adding to the whole number of free persons, including those bound to service for a term of years, and excluding Indians not taxed, three fifths of all other persons. The actual enumeration shall be made within three years after the first meeting of the Congress of the United States, and within every subsequent term of ten years, in such manner as they shall by law direct. The number of representatives shall not exceed one for every thirty thousand, but each State shall have at least one representative; and until such enumeration shall be made, the State of New Hampshire shall be entitled to choose three; Massachusetts, eight; Rhode Island and Providence Plantations, one; Connecticut, five; New York, six; New Jersey, four; Pennsylvania, eight; Delaware, one; Maryland, six; Virginia, ten; North Carolina, five; South Carolina, five; and Georgia, three.

(Clause 4.) When vacancies happen in the representation from any State, the executive authority thereof shall issue writs of election to fill such vacancies.

(Clause 5.) The House of Representatives shall choose their speaker and other officers and shall have the sole power of impeachment.

SEC. III. (Clause 1.) The Senate of the United States shall be composed of two senators from each State, chosen by the legislatures thereof, for six years; and each senator shall have one vote.

(Clause 2.) Immediately after they shall be assembled in consequence of the first election, they shall be divided as equally as may be into three classes. The seats of the senators of the first class shall be vacated at the expiration of the second year, of the second class, at the expiration of the fourth year, and of the third class, at the expiration of the sixth year, so that one third may be chosen every second year; and if vacancies happen by resignation, or otherwise, during the recess of the legislature of any State, the executive thereof may make temporary appointments until the next meeting of the legislature, which shall then fill such vacancies.

(Clause 3.) No person shall be a senator who shall not have attained to the age of thirty years, and been nine years a citizen of the United States, and who shall not, when elected, be an inhabitant of that State for which he shall be chosen.

(Clause 4.) The Vice-President of the United States shall be president of the Senate, but shall have no vote, unless they be equally divided.

(Clause 5.) The Senate shall choose their other officers, and also a president *pro tempore*, in the absence of the Vice-President, or when he shall exercise the office of President of the United States.

(Clause 6.) The Senate shall have the sole power to try all impeachments ; when sitting for that purpose they shall be on oath or affirmation. When the President of the United States is tried, the Chief Justice shall preside ; and no person shall be convicted without the concurrence of two thirds of the members present.

(Clause 7.) Judgment in cases of impeachment shall not be extended further than to removal from office, and disqualification to hold and enjoy any office of honor, trust, or profit, under the United States ; but the party convicted shall nevertheless be liable and subject to indictment, trial, judgment, and punishment, according to law.

SEC. IV. (Clause 1.) The times, places and manner of holding elections for senators and representatives shall be prescribed in each State by the legislature thereof; but the Congress may at any time, by law, make or alter such regulations, except as to the places of choosing senators.

(Clause 2.) The Congress shall assemble at least once in every year, and such meeting shall be on the first Monday in December, unless they shall by law appoint a different day.

SEC. V. (Clause 1.) Each house shall be the judge of the elections, returns, and qualifications of its own members, and a majority of each shall constitute a quorum to do business ; but a smaller number may adjourn from day to day, and may be authorized to compel the attendance of absent members, in such manner, and under such penalties, as each house may provide.

(Clause 2.) Each house may determine the rules of its proceedings, punish its members for disorderly behavior, and with the concurrence of two thirds expel a member.

(Clause 3.) Each house shall keep a journal of its proceedings, and from time to time publish the same excepting such parts as may in their judgment require secrecy, and the yeas and nays of the members of either house on any question shall, at the desire of one fifth of those present, be entered on the journal.

(Clause 4.) Neither house, during the session of Congress, shall, without the consent of the other, adjourn for more than three days, nor to any other place than that in which the two houses shall be sitting.

SEC. VI. (Clause 1.) The senators and representatives shall receive a compensation for their services, to be ascertained by law, and paid out of the treasury of the United States. They shall in all cases, except treason, felony, and breach of peace, be privileged from arrest during their attendance at the session of their respective houses, and in going to and returning from the same ; and for any speech or debate in either house, they shall not be questioned in any other place.

(Clause 2.) No senator or representative shall, during the time for which he was elected, be appointed to any civil office under the authority of the United States, which shall have been created, or the emoluments whereof shall have been increased, during such time ; and no person holding any office under the United States shall be a member of either house during his continuance in office.

SEC. VII. (Clause 1.) All bills for raising revenue shall originate in the House of Representatives ; but the Senate may propose or concur with amendments, as on other bills.

(Clause 2.) Every bill which shall have passed the House of Representatives and the Senate, shall, before it becomes a law, be presented to the President of the United States ; if he approve, he shall sign it, but if not, he shall return it, with his objections, to that house in which it shall have originated, who shall enter the objections at large on their journal, and proceed to reconsider it. If, after such reconsideration, two thirds of that house shall agree to pass the bill, it shall be sent, together with the objections, to the other house, by which it shall likewise be reconsidered, and, if approved by two thirds of that house, it shall become a law. But in all such cases the votes of both houses shall be determined by yeas and nays, and the names of the persons voting for and against the bill shall be entered on the journal of each house, respectively. If any bill shall not be returned by the President within ten days (Sundays excepted) after it shall have been presented to him, the same shall be a law, in like manner as if he had signed it, unless the Congress, by their adjournment, prevent its return, in which case it shall not be a law.

(Clause 3.) Every order, resolution, or vote, to which the concurrence of the Senate and House of Representatives may be necessary (except on a case of adjournment), shall be presented to the President of the United States; and before the same shall take effect shall be approved by him, or, being disapproved by him, shall be repassed by two thirds of the Senate and House of Representatives, according to the rules and limitations prescribed in the case of a bill.

SEC. VIII. (Clause 1.) The Congress shall have power to lay and collect taxes, duties, imposts, and excises, to pay the debts and provide for the common defense and general welfare of the United States; but all duties, imposts, and excises shall be uniform throughout the United States;

(Clause 2.) To borrow money on the credit of the United States;

(Clause 3.) To regulate commerce with foreign nations, and among the several States, and with the Indian tribes;

(Clause 4.) To establish a uniform rule of naturalization, and uniform laws on the subject of bankruptcies, throughout the United States;

(Clause 5.) To coin money, regulate the value thereof, and of foreign coin, and fix the standard of weights and measures;

(Clause 6.) To provide for the punishment of counterfeiting the securities and current coin of the United States;

(Clause 7.) To establish postoffices and postroads;

(Clause 8) To promote the progress of science and

useful arts, by securing, for limited times, to authors and inventors, the exclusive right to their respective writings and discoveries;

(Clause 9.) To constitute tribunals inferior to the Supreme Court;

(Clause 10.) To define and punish piracies and felonies committed on the high seas, and offenses against the law of nations;

(Clause 11.) To declare war, grant letters of marque and reprisal, and make rules concerning captures on land and water;

(Clause 12.) To raise and support armies; but no appropriation of money to that use shall be for a longer term than two years;

(Clause 13.) To provide and maintain a navy;

(Clause 14.) To make rules for the government and regulation of the land and naval forces;

(Clause 15.) To provide for calling forth the militia to execute the laws of the Union, suppress insurrections, and repel invasions;

(Clause 16.) To provide for organizing, arming, and disciplining the militia, and for governing such part of them as may be employed in the service of the United States; reserving to the States respectively the appointment of the officers, and the authority of training the militia, according to the discipline prescribed by Congress;

(Clause 17.) To exercise exclusive legislation in all cases whatsoever, over such district (not exceeding ten miles square), as may, by cession of particular States, and the acceptance of Congress, become the seat of the government of the United States, and to exercise like authority over all places, purchased by consent of the legislature of the State in which the same shall be, for the erection of forts, magazines, arsenals, dockyards, and other needful buildings; and,

(Clause 18.) To make all laws which shall be necessary and proper for carrying into execution the foregoing powers, and all other powers vested by this Constitution in the government of the United States, or in any department or officer thereof.

SEC. IX. (Clause 1.) The migration or importation of such persons, as any of the States, now existing, shall think proper to admit, shall not be prohibited by the Congress, prior to the year one thousand eight hundred and eight, but a tax or duty may be imposed on such importation, not exceeding ten dollars for each person.

(Clause 2.) The privilege of the writ of *habeas corpus* shall not be suspended, unless when in cases of rebellion or invasion, the public safety may require it.

(Clause 3.) No bill of attainder, or *ex post facto* law, shall be passed.

(Clause 4.) No capitation or other direct tax shall be laid, unless in proportion to the *census* or enumeration, hereinbefore directed to be taken.

(Clause 5.) No tax or duty shall be laid on articles exported from any State. No preference shall be given by any regulation of commerce or revenue, to the ports of one State over those of another, nor shall vessels bound to, or from, one State, be obliged to enter, clear, or pay duties, in another.

(Clause 6.) No money shall be drawn from the Treasury, but in consequence of appropriations made by law; and a regular statement and account of the receipts and expenditures of all public money shall be published, from time to time.

(Clause 7.) No title of nobility shall be granted by the United States: and no person, holding any office of profit or trust under them, shall, without the consent of Congress, accept of any present, emolument, office, or title, of any kind whatever, from any king, prince, or foreign state.

SEC. X. (Clause 1.) No State shall enter into any treaty, alliance, or confederation; grant letters of marque and reprisal; coin money; emit bills of credit; make anything but gold and silver coin a tender in payment of debts; pass any bill of attainder, *ex post facto* law, or law impairing the obligation of contracts, or grant any title of nobility.

(Clause 2.) No State shall, without the consent of the Congress, lay any imposts or duties on imports or exports, except what may be absolutely necessary for executing its inspection laws; and the net produce of all duties and imposts, laid by any State on imports or exports, shall be for the use of the Treasury of the United States; and all such laws shall be subject to the revision and control of the Congress.

(Clause 3.) No State shall, without the consent of Congress lay any duty of tonnage, keep troops, or ships of war, in time of peace, enter into any agreement or compact with another State, or with a foreign power, or engage in war, unless actually invaded, or in such imminent danger as will not admit of delay.

ARTICLE II.

EXECUTIVE DEPARTMENT.

SECTION I. (Clause 1.) The executive power shall be vested in a President of the United States of America. He shall hold his office during the term of four years, and, together with the Vice-President, chosen for the same term, be elected as follows:

(Clause 2.) Each State shall appoint, in such manner as the legislature thereof may direct, a number of electors, equal to the whole number of senators and representatives to which the State may be entitled in the Congress; but no senator or representative, or person holding an office of trust, or profit under the United States, shall be appointed an elector.

*(Clause 3.) The electors shall meet in their respective States, and vote by ballot for two persons, of whom one, at least, shall not be an inhabitant of the same State with themselves. And they shall make a list of all the persons voted for and of the number of votes for each; which list they sign and certify, and transmit, sealed, to the seat of the government of the United States, directed to the President of the Senate. The President of the Senate shall, in the presence of the Senate and House of Representatives, open the certificates, and the votes shall then be counted. The person having the greatest number of votes shall be the President, if such number be a majority of the whole number of electors appointed; and if there be more than one who have such a majority, and have an equal number of votes, then the House of Representatives shall immediately choose, by ballot, one of them, for President; and if no person have a majority, then, from the five highest on the list, the said house shall, in like manner, choose the President. But in choosing the President, the vote shall be taken by States, the representation from each State having one vote; a quorum for this purpose shall consist of a number of members, from two thirds of the States, and a majority of all the States shall be necessary to a choice. In every case, after the choice of the President, the person having the greatest number of votes of the electors shall be the Vice-President. But if there should remain two or more who have

---
*This clause has been superceded by the XIIth Amendment.

equal votes, the Senate shall choose from them, by ballot, the Vice-President.

(Clause 4.) The Congress may determine the time of choosing the electors, and the day on which they shall give their votes; which day shall be the same throughout the United States.

(Clause 5.) No person, except a natural-born citizen, or a citizen of the United States at the time of the adoption of this Constitution, shall be eligible to the office of President; neither shall any person be eligible to that office who shall not have attained to the age of thirty-five years, and been fourteen years a resident within the United States.

(Clause 6.) In case of the removal of the President from office, or of his death, resignation, or inability to discharge the powers and duties of the said office, the same shall devolve on the Vice-President, and the Congress may by law provide for the case of removal, death, resignation, or inability both of the President and Vice-President, declaring what officer shall then act as President; and such officer shall act accordingly, until the disability be removed or a President shall be elected.

(Clause 7.) The President shall, at stated times, receive for his service, a compensation which shall neither be increased nor diminished during the period for which he shall have been elected, and he shall not receive within that period, any other emolument from the United States, or any of them.

(Clause 8.) Before he enter on the execution of his office he shall take the following oath or affirmation: I do solemnly swear (or affirm) that I will faithfully execute the office of President of the United States, and will, to the best of my ability, preserve, protect, and defend the Constitution of the United States.

SEC. II. (Clause 1.) The President shall be commander-in-chief of the army and navy of the United States, and of the militia of the several States, when called into the actual service of the United States; he may require the opinion, in writing, of the principal officer in each of the executive departments, upon any subject relating to the duties of their respective offices, and he shall have power to grant reprieves and pardons for offenses against the United States, except in cases of impeachment.

(Clause 2.) He shall have power, by and with the advice and consent of the Senate, to make treaties, provided two thirds of the senators present concur, and he shall nominate, and by and with the advice and consent of the Senate, shall appoint ambassadors, other public ministers, and consuls, judges of the Supreme Court, and all other officers of the United States, whose appointments are not herein otherwise provided for, and which shall be established by law; but the Congress may by law vest the appointment of such inferior officers, as they think proper, in the President alone, in the courts of law, or in the heads of departments.

(Clause 3.) The President shall have power to fill up all vacancies that may happen during the recess of the Senate, by granting commissions which shall expire at the end of their next session.

SEC. III. He shall, from time to time, give to the Congress information of the state of the Union, and recommend to their consideration such measures as he shall judge necessary and expedient; he may, on extraordinary occasions, convene both houses, or either of them, and in case of disagreement between them with respect to the time of adjournment, he may adjourn them to such time as he shall think proper; he shall receive ambassadors and other public ministers; he shall take care that the laws be faithfully executed, and shall commission all the officers in the United States.

SEC. IV. The President, Vice-President, and all civil officers of the United States, shall be removed from office, on impeachment for, and conviction of, treason, bribery, or other high crimes and misdemeanors.

ARTICLE III.

JUDICIAL DEPARTMENT.

SECTION I. The judicial power of the United States shall be vested in one Supreme Court, and in such inferior courts as the Congress may, from time to time, ordain and establish. The judges, both of the Supreme and inferior courts, shall hold their offices during good behavior, and shall, at stated times, receive for their services, a compensation which shall not be diminished during their continuance in office.

SEC. II. (Clause 1.) The judicial power shall extend to all cases in law and equity arising under this Constitution, the laws of the United States, and treaties made, or which shall be made, under their authority; to all cases affecting ambassadors, other public ministers, and consuls; to all cases of admiralty and maritime jurisdiction; to controversies to which the United States shall be a party; to controversies between two or more States, between a State and citizens of another State, between citizens of different States, between citizens of the same State claiming lands under grants of different States, and between a State, or the citizens thereof, and foreign States, citizens, or subjects.

(Clause 2.) In all cases affecting ambassadors, other public ministers, and consuls, and those in which a State shall be a party, the Supreme Court shall have original jurisdiction. In all the other cases before mentioned, the Supreme Court shall have appellate jurisdiction, both as to law and fact, with such exceptions, and under such regulations, as the Congress shall make.

(Clause 3.) The trial of all crimes, except in cases of impeachment, shall be by jury; and such trial shall be held in the State where the said crimes shall have been committed; but when not committed within any State, the trial shall be at such place, or places, as the Congress may by law have directed.

SEC. III. (Clause 1.) Treason against the United States shall consist only in levying war against them, or in adhering to their enemies, giving them aid and comfort. No person shall be convicted of treason, unless on the testimony of two witnesses to the same overt act, or on confession in open court.

(Clause 2.) The Congress shall have power to declare the punishment of treason, but no attainder of treason shall work corruption of blood, or forfeiture, except during the life of the person attainted.

ARTICLE IV.

SECTION I. Full faith and credit shall be given in each State to the public acts, records, and judicial proceedings of every other State. And the Congress may, by general laws, prescribe the manner in which such acts, records, and proceedings shall be proved, and the effect thereof.

SEC. II. (Clause 1.) The citizens of each State shall be entitled to all privileges and immunities of citizens in the several states.

(Clause 2.) A person charged in any State with treason, felony, or other crime, who shall flee from justice, and be found in another State, shall, on demand of the executive authority of the State from which he fled, be delivered up, to be removed to the State having jurisdiction of the crime.

(Clause 3.) No person held to service or labor in one State, under the laws thereof, escaping into another, shall, in consequence of any law or regulation therein, be discharged from such service or labor, but shall be delivered up on claim of the party to whom such service or labor may be due.

SEC. III. (Clause 1.) New States may be admitted by the Congress into this Union, but no new State shall be formed or erected within the jurisdiction of any other State; nor any State be formed by the junction of two or more States, or parts of States, without the consent of the legislatures of the States concerned, as well as of the Congress.

(Clause 2.) The Congress shall have power to dispose of and make all needful rules and regulations respecting the territory, or other property, belonging to the United States; and nothing in this Constitution shall be so construed as to prejudice any claims of the United States, or of any particular State.

SEC. IV. The United States shall guarantee to every State in this Union a republican form of government, and shall protect each of them against invasion; and, on application of the legislature, or of the executive (when the legislature cannot be convened), against domestic violence.

ARTICLE V.

The Congress, whenever two thirds of both houses shall deem it necessary, shall propose amendments to this Constitution, or on the application of the legislatures of two thirds of the several States, shall call a convention for proposing amendments, which, in either case, shall be valid to all intents and purposes, as part of this Constitution, when ratified by the legislatures of three fourths of the several States, or by conventions in three fourths thereof, as the one or the other mode of ratification may be proposed by the Congress: *Provided*, that no Amendment, which may be made prior to the year one thousand eight hundred and eight shall in any manner affect the first and fourth clauses in the ninth section of the first article, and that no State, without its consent, shall be deprived of its equal suffrage in the Senate.

ARTICLE VI.

(Clause 1.) All debts contracted, and engagements entered into, before the adoption of this Constitution, shall be as valid against the United States, under this Constitution, as under the Confederation.

(Clause 2.) This Constitution, and the laws of the United States which shall be made in pursuance thereof, and all treaties made, or which shall be made, under the authority of the United States, shall be the supreme law of the land ; and the judges in every State shall be bound thereby, anything in the Constitution or laws of any State to the contrary notwithstanding.

(Clause 3.) The senators and representatives before mentioned, and the members of the several State legislatures, and all executive and judicial officers, both of the United States, and of the several States, shall be bound, by oath or affirmation, to support this Constitution ; but no religious test shall ever be required as a qualification to any office or public trust under the United States.

ARTICLE VII.

The ratification of the conventions of nine States shall be sufficient for the establishment of this Con-

stitution between the States so ratifying the same.
Done in convention by the unanimous consent of the States present, the seventeenth day of September, in the year of our Lord one thousand seven hundred and eighty-seven, and of the Independence of the United States of America the twelfth.

AMENDMENTS

To the Constitution of the United States, Ratified according to the Provisions of the Fifth Article of the foregoing Constitution.

ARTICLE I.

Congress shall make no law respecting an establishment of religion, or prohibiting the free exercise thereof, or abridging the freedom of speech, or of the press; or the right of the people peaceably to assemble, and to petition the Government for a redress of grievances. (1791.)

ARTICLE II.

A well-regulated militia being necessary to the security of a free State, the right of the people to keep and bear arms shall not be infringed. (1791.)

ARTICLE III.

No soldier shall, in time of peace, be quartered in any house, without the consent of the owner, nor, in time of war, but in a manner to be prescribed by law. (1791.)

ARTICLE IV.

The right of the people to be secure in their persons, houses, papers and effects, against unreasonable searches and seizures, shall not be violated; and no warrants shall issue, but upon probable cause, supported by oath or affirmation, and particularly describing the place to be searched, and the persons or things to be seized. (1791.)

ARTICLE V.

No person shall be held to answer for a capital or otherwise infamous crime, unless on a presentment or indictment of a grand jury, except in cases arising in the land or naval forces, or in the militia, when in actual service, in time of war, or public danger : nor shall any person be subject, for the same offense, to be twice put in jeopardy of life or limb ; nor shall be compelled in any criminal case, to be a witness against himself, nor be deprived of life, liberty, or property, without due process of law, nor shall private property be taken for public use, without just compensation. (1791.)

ARTICLE VI.

In all criminal prosecutions, the accused shall enjoy the right to a speedy and public trial, by an impartial jury of the State and district wherein the crime shall have been committed, which district shall have been previously ascertained by law, and to be informed of the nature and cause of the accusation ; to be confronted with the witnesses against him ; to have compulsory process for obtaining witnesses in his favor ; and to have the assistance of counsel for his defense. (1791.)

ARTICLE VII.

In suits at common law, where the value in controversy shall exceed twenty dollars, the right of trial by jury shall be preserved ; and no fact, tried by a jury, shall be otherwise re-examined in any court of the United States, than according to the rules of the common law. (1791.)

ARTICLE VIII.

Excessive bail shall not be required, nor excessive fines imposed, nor cruel and unusual punishments inflicted. (1791.)

ARTICLE IX.

The enumeration in the Constitution of certain rights shall not be construed to deny or disparage others retained by the people. (1791.)

ARTICLE X.

The powers not delegated to the United States by the Constitution, nor prohibited by it to the States, are reserved to the States respectively, or to the people. (1791.)

ARTICLE XI.

The judicial power of the United States shall not be construed to extend to any suit in law or equity, commenced or prosecuted against one of the United States by citizens of another State, or by citizens or subjects of any foreign State. (1798.)

ARTICLE XII.

(Clause 1.) The electors shall meet in their respective States, and vote by ballot for President and Vice-President, one of whom, at least, shall not be an inhabitant of the same State with themselves; they shall name in their ballots the person voted for as President; and in distinct ballots the person voted for as Vice-President; and they shall make distinct lists of all persons voted for as President and of all persons voted for as Vice-President, and of the number of votes for each, which lists, they shall sign, and certify, and transmit, sealed, to the seat of the government of the United States, directed to the president of the Senate; the president of the Senate shall, in the presence of the Senate and House of Representatives, open all the certificates, and the votes shall then be counted; the person having the greatest number of votes for President shall be the President, if such number be a majority of the whole number of electors appointed; and if no person have such majority, then, from the persons having the highest numbers, not exceeding three, on the list of those voted for as President, the House of Representatives shall choose immediately, by ballot, the President, but in choosing the President, the votes shall be taken by States, the representation from each State having one vote; a quorum for this purpose shall consist of a member or members from two thirds of the States, and a majority of all the States shall be necessary to a choice. And if the House of Representatives shall not choose a President, whenever the right to choose shall devolve upon them, before the fourth day of March next following, then the Vice-President shall act as President as in the case of the death, or other Constitutional disability of the President.

(Clause 2.) The person having the greatest number of votes as Vice-President shall be the Vice-President, if such number be a majority of the whole number of electors appointed; and if no person have a majority, then, from the two highest numbers on the list, the Senate shall choose the Vice-President; a quorum for the purpose shall consist of two thirds of the whole number of senators; a majority of the whole number shall be necessary to a choice.

(Clause 3.) But no person Constitutionally ineligible to the office of President, shall be eligible to that of Vice-President of the United States. (1804.)

Article XIII.

(Clause 1.) Neither slavery nor involuntary servitude, except as a punishment for crime, whereof the party shall have been duly convicted, shall exist within the United States, or any place subject to their jurisdiction.

(Clause 2.) Congress shall have power to enforce this article by appropriate legislation. (1865)

ARTICLE XIV.

(Clause 1.) All persons born or naturalized in the United States, and subject to the jurisdiction thereof, are citizens of the United States and of the State wherein they reside. No State shall make or enforce any law which shall abridge the privileges or immunites of citizens of the United States; nor shall any State deprive any person of life, liberty, or property, without due process of law, nor deny to any person within its jurisdiction the equal protection of the laws.

(Clause 2.) Representatives shall be apportioned among the several States according to their respective numbers, counting the whole number of persons in each State, excluding Indians not taxed. But when the right to vote at any election for the choice of electors for President and Vice-President of the United States, representatives in Congress, the executive and judicial officers of a State, or the members of the legislature thereof, is denied to any of the male inhabitants of such State, being twenty-one years of age, and citizens of the United States, or in any way abridged, except for participation in rebellion, or other crime, the basis of representation therein shall be reduced in the proportion which the number of such male citizens shall bear to the whole number of male citizens twenty-one years of age, in such State.

(Clause 3.) No person shall be a senator or representative in Congress or elector of President and

Vice-President, or hold any office, civil or military, under the United States, or under any State, who, having previously taken an oath as a member of Congress, or as an officer of the United States, or as a member of any State legislature, or an executive or judicial officer of any State, to support the Constitution of the United States, shall have engaged in insurrection or rebellion against the same, or given aid or comfort to the enemies thereof. But Congress may, by a vote of two thirds of each house, remove such disability.

(Clause 4.) The validity of the public debt of the United States, authorized by law, including debts incurred for payment of pensions and bounties for services in suppressing insurrection or rebellion, shall not be questioned. But neither the United States nor any State shall assume or pay any debt or obligation incurred in aid of insurrection or rebellion against the United States, or any claim for the loss or emancipation of any slave, but all such debts, obligations, and claims, shall be held illegal and void.

(Clause 5.) The Congress shall have power to enforce, by appropriate legislation, the provisions of this article. (1868.)

Article XV.

(Clause 1.) The right of citizens of the United States to vote shall not be denied or abridged by the United States or by any State, on account of race, color, or previous condition of servitude.

(Clause 2.) The Congress shall have power to enforce this article by appropriate legislation. (1870.)

CONSTITUTION OF PENNSYLVANIA.

[This Constitution went into operation on January 1, 1874, except wherein otherwise provided therein.

PREAMBLE.

We, the people of the Commonwealth of Pennsylvania, grateful to Almighty God for the blessings of civil and religious liberty, and humbly invoking His guidance, do ordain and establish this Constitution.

ARTICLE I.

DECLARATION OF RIGHTS.

That the general, great and essential principles of liberty and free government may be recognized and unalterably established, we declare that

SEC. 1. All men are born equally free and independent, and have certain inherent and indefeasible rights, among which are those of enjoying and defending life and liberty, of acquiring, possessing, and protecting property and reputation, and of pursuing their own happiness.

SEC. 2. All power is inherent in the people, and all free governments are founded on their authority and instituted for their peace, safety, and happiness. For the advancement of these ends, they have at all times an inalienable and indefeasible right to alter, reform, or abolish their government in such manner as they may think proper.

SEC. 3. All men have a natural and indefeasible

right to worship Almighty God according to the dictates of their own consciences; no man can of right be compelled to attend, erect, or support any place of worship, or to maintain any ministry against his consent; no human authority can, in any case whatever, control or interfere with the rights of conscience, aud no preference shall ever be given by law to any religious establishments or modes of worship.

SEC. 4. No person who acknowledges the being of a God, and a future state of rewards and punishments, shall, on account of his religious sentiments, be disqualified to hold any office or place of trust or profit under this Commonwealth.

SEC. 5. Elections shall be free and equal; and no power, civil or military, shall at any time interfere to prevent the free exercise of the right of suffrage.

SEC. 6. Trial by jury shall be as heretofore, and the right thereof remain inviolate.

SEC. 7. The printing press shall be free to every person who may undertake to examine the proceedings of the legislature, or any branch of government, and no law shall ever be made to restrain the right thereof. The free communication of thoughts and opinions is one of the invaluable rights of man, and every citizen may freely speak, write, and print on any subject, being responsible for the abuse of that liberty. No conviction shall be had in any prosecution for the publication of papers relating to the official conduct of officers or men in public capacity, or to any other matter proper for public investigation or information, where the fact that such publication was not maliciously or negligently made shall be established to the satisfaction of the jury; and in all indictments for libel, the jury shall have the right to determine the law and the facts under the direction of the court, as in other cases.

SEC. 8. The people shall be secure in their persons, houses, papers, and possessions from unreasonable searches and seizures, and no warrant to search any place or to seize any person or things shall issue without describing them as nearly as may be, nor without probable cause, supported by oath or affirmation, subscribed to by the affiant.

SEC. 9. In all criminal prosecutions the accused hath a right to be heard by himself and his counsel, to demand the nature and cause of the accusation against him, to meet the witnesses face to face, to have compulsory process for obtaining witnesses in his favor, and, in prosecutions by indictment or information, a speedy public trial by an impartial jury of the vicinage; he cannot be compelled to give evidence against himself, nor can he be deprived of his life, liberty, or property, unless by the judgment of his peers or the law of the land.

SEC. 10. No person shall, for any indictable offense, be proceeded against criminally by information, except in cases arising in the land or naval forces, or in the militia, when in actual service, in time of war or public danger, or by leave of the court, for oppression or misdemeanor in office. No person shall, for the same offense, be twice put in jeopardy of life or limb; nor shall private property be taken or applied to public use, without authority of law and without just compensation being first made or secured.

SEC. 11. All courts shall be open, and every man for an injury done him in his lands, goods, person, or reputation, shall have remedy by due course of law, and right and justice administered without sale, denial, or delay. Suits may be brought against the

Commonwealth in such manner, in such courts, and in such cases as the legislature may by law direct.

SEC. 12. No power of suspending laws shall be exercised unless by the legislature, or by its authority.

SEC. 13. Excessive bail shall not be required, nor excessive fines imposed, nor cruel punishments inflicted.

SEC. 14. All prisoners shall be bailable by sufficient sureties, unless for capital offenses, when the proof is evident or presumption great; and the privilege of the writ of *habeas corpus* shall not be suspended, unless when in case of rebellion or invasion the public safety may require it.

SEC. 15. No commission of oyer or terminer or jail delivery shall be issued.

SEC. 16. The person of a debtor, where there is not strong presumption of fraud, shall not be continued in prison after delivering up his estate for the benefit of his creditors, in such manner as shall be prescribed by law.

SEC. 17. No *ex post facto* law, nor any law impairing the obligation of contracts, or making irrevocable any grant of special privileges or immunities, shall be passed.

SEC. 18. No person shall be attainted of treason or felony by the legislature.

SEC. 19. No attainder shall work corruption of blood, nor, except during the life of the offender, forfeiture of estate to the Commonwealth. The estate of such persons as shall destroy their own lives shall descend or vest as in cases of natural death, and if any person shall be killed by casualty there shall be no forfeiture by reason thereof.

SEC. 20. The citizens have a right in a peaceable manner to assemble together for their common good, and to apply to those invested with the powers of government for redress of grievances or other proper purposes by petition, address, or remonstrance.

SEC. 21. The right of the citizens to bear arms in defense of themselves and the State shall not be questioned.

SEC. 22. No standing army shall, in time of peace, be kept up without the consent of the legislature, and the military shall in all cases and at all times be in strict subordination to the civil power.

SEC. 23. No soldier shall in time of peace be quartered in any house without the consent of the owner, nor in time of war but in a manner to be prescribed by law.

SEC. 24. The legislature shall not grant any title of nobility or hereditary distinction, nor create any office, the appointment to which shall be for a longer term than during good behavior.

SEC. 25. Emigration from the State shall not be prohibited.

SEC. 26. To guard against transgressions of the high powers which we have delegated, we declare that everything in this article is excepted out of the general powers of government and shall forever remain inviolate.

ARTICLE II.

THE LEGISLATURE.

SEC. 1. The legislative power of this Commonwealth shall be vested in a General Assembly, which shall consist of a Senate and a House of Representatives.

SEC. 2. Members of the General Assembly shall be chosen at the general election every second year. Their term of service shall begin on the first day of December next after their election. Whenever a vacancy shall occur in either house, the presiding officer thereof shall issue a writ of election to fill such vacancy for the remainder of the term.

SEC. 3. Senators shall be elected for the term of four years, and representatives for the term of two years.

Sec. 4. The General Assembly shall meet at twelve o'clock, noon, on the first Tuesday of January every second year, and at other times when convened by the Governor, but shall hold no adjourned annual session after the year one thousand eight hundred and seventy-eight. In case of a vacancy in the office of United States senator from this Commonwealth, in a recess between sessions, the Governor shall convene the two houses, by proclamation on notice not exceeding sixty days, to fill the same.

SEC. 5. Senators shall be at least twenty-five years of age, and representatives twenty-one years of age. They shall have been citizens and inhabitants of the State four years, and inhabitants of their respective districts one year next before their election (unless absent on the public business of the United States, or of this State), and shall reside in their respective districts during their terms of service.

SEC. 6. No senator or representative shall, during the time for which he shall have been elected, be appointed to any civil office under this Commonwealth, and no member of Congress, or other person holding any office (except of attorney-at-law or in the militia), under the United States, or this Commonwealth, shall be a member of either house during his continuance in office.

SEC. 7. No person hereafter convicted of embezzlement of public moneys, bribery, perjury, or other infamous crime, shall be eligible to the General Assembly, or capable of holding any office of trust or profit in this Commonwealth.

SEC. 8. The members of the General Assembly shall receive such salary and mileage for regular and special sessions as shall be fixed by law, and no other compensation whatever, whether for service upon committee or otherwise. No member of either house shall, during the term for which he may have been elected, receive any increase of salary or mileage, under any law passed during such term.

SEC. 9. The Senate shall, at the beginning and close of each regular session, and at such other times as may be necessary, elect one of its members president *pro tempore*, who shall perform the duties of the Lieutenant-Governor, in any case of absence or disability of that officer, and whenever the said office of the Lieutenant-Governor shall be vacant. The House of Representatives shall elect one of its members as speaker. Each house shall choose its other officers, and shall judge of the election and qualifications of its members.

SEC. 10. A majority of each house shall constitute a quorum, but a smaller number may adjourn from day to day, and compel the attendance of absent members.

SEC. 11. Each house shall have power to determine the rules of its proceedings, and punish its members or other persons for contempt or disorderly behavior in its presence, to enforce obedience to its process, to protect its members against violence, or offers of bribes or private solicitation, and with the concurrence of two thirds, to expel a member, but not a second time for the same cause, and shall have all other powers necessary for the legislature of a free State. A member expelled for corruption shall not thereafter be eligible to either house, and punishment for contempt or disorderly behavior shall not bar an indictment for the same offense.

SEC. 12. Each house shall keep a journal of its proceedings, and from time to time publish the same, except such parts as require secrecy, and the yeas and nays of the members on any question shall, at the desire of any two of them, be entered on the journal.

SEC. 13. The sessions of each house, and of committees of the whole, shall be open, unless when the business is such as ought to be kept secret.

SEC. 14. Neither house shall, without the consent of the other, adjourn for more than three days, nor to any other place than that in which the two houses shall be sitting.

SEC. 15. The members of the General Assembly shall in all cases except treason, felony, violation of their oath of office, and breach or surety of the peace, be privileged from arrest during their attendance at the sessions of their respective houses and in going to and returning from the same; and for any speech or debate in either house they shall not be questioned in any other place.

SEC. 16. The State shall be divided into fifty senatorial districts of compact and contiguous territory as nearly equal in population as may be, and each district shall be entitled to elect one senator. Each county containing one or more ratios of population shall be entitled to one senator for each ratio, and to an additional senator for a surplus of population exceeding three fifths of a ratio, but no county shall form a separate district unless it shall contain four fifths of a ratio, except where the adjoining counties are each entitled to one or more senators, when such county may be assigned a senator on less than four fifths and exceeding one half of a ratio; and no county shall be divided unless entitled to two or more senators. No city or county shall be entitled to separate representation exceeding one sixth of the whole number of senators. No ward, borough, or township shall be divided in the formation of a district. The senatorial ratio shall be ascertained by dividing the whole population of the State by the number fifty.

SEC. 17. The members of the House of Representatives shall be apportioned among the several counties, on a ratio obtained by dividing the population of the State, as ascertained by the most recent United States census, by two hundred. Every county containing less than five ratios shall have one representative for every full ratio, and an additional representative when the surplus exceeds half a ratio; but each county shall have at least one representative. Every county containing five ratios or more shall have one representative for every full ratio. Every city containing a population equal to a ratio shall elect separately its proportion of the representatives allotted to the county in which it is located. Every city entitled to more than four representatives, and every county having over one hundred thousand inhabitants, shall be divided into districts of compact and contiguous territory, each district to elect its proportion of representatives according to its population, but no district shall elect more than four representatives.

SEC. 18. The General Assembly at its first session after the adoption of this Constitution, and immediately after each United States decennial census, shall apportion the State into senatorial and representative districts, agreeably to the provisions of the two next preceding sections.

ARTICLE III.

LEGISLATION.

SEC. 1. No law shall be passed except by bill, and

no bill shall be so altered or amended, on its passage through either house, as to change its original purpose.

SEC. 2. No bill shall be considered unless referred to a committee, returned therefrom, and printed for the use of the members.

SEC 3. No bills, except general appropriation bills, shall be passed containing more than one subject, which shall be clearly expressed in its title.

SEC. 4. Every bill shall be read at length on three different days, in each house; all amendments made thereto shall be printed for the use of the members before the final vote is taken on the bill, and no bill shall become a law, unless on its final passage the vote be taken by yeas and nays, the names of the persons voting for and against the same be entered on the journal, and a majority of the members elected to each house be recorded thereon as voting in its favor.

SEC. 5. No amendments to bills by one house shall be concurred in by the other, except by the vote of a majority of the members elected thereto taken by yeas and nays, and the names of those voting for and against recorded upon the journal thereof; and reports of committees of conference shall be adopted in either house only by the vote of a majority of the members elected thereto, taken by yeas and nays, and the names of those voting recorded upon the journals.

SEC. 6. No law shall be revived, amended, or the provisions thereof extended or conferred, by reference to its title only, but so much thereof as is revived, amended, extended, or conferred, shall be re-enacted, and published at length.

SEC. 7. The General Assembly shall not pass any local or special law authorizing the creation, extension, or impairing of liens; regulating the affairs of counties, cities, townships, wards, boroughs, or school districts; changing the names of persons or places; changing the venue in civil or criminal cases; authorizing the laying out, opening, altering, or maintaining roads, highways, streets, or alleys; relating to ferries or bridges, or incorporating ferry or bridge companies, except for the erection of bridges crossing streams which form boundaries between this and any other State; vacating roads, town plats, streets, or alleys; relating to cemeteries, grave-yards, or public grounds not of the State; authorizing the adoption or legitimation of children; locating or changing county seats; erecting new counties, or changing county lines; incorporating cities, towns, or villages, or changing their charters; for the opening and conducting of elections, or fixing or changing the place of voting; granting divorces; erecting new townships or boroughs; changing township lines, borough limits, or school districts; creating offices, or prescribing the powers and duties of officers in counties, cities, boroughs, townships, election, or school districts; changing the law of descent or succession; regulating the practice or jurisdiction of, or changing the rules of evidence in, any judicial proceeding or inquiry before courts, aldermen, justices of the peace, sheriffs, commissioners, arbitrators, auditors, masters in chancery, or other tribunals, or providing or changing methods for the collection of debts, or the enforcing of judgments, or prescribing the effect of judicial sales of real estate; regulating the fees, or extending the powers and duties of aldermen, justices of the peace, magistrates, or constables; regulating the management of public schools, the building or repairing of school-houses, and the raising of money for such purposes; fixing the rate of interest; affecting the estates of minors or persons under disability, except after due notice to all parties in interest, to be recited in the special enactment; remitting fines, penalties, and forfeitures, or refunding moneys legally paid into the treasury; exempting property from taxation; regulating labor, trade, mining, or manufacturing; creating corporations, or amending, renewing, or extending the charters thereof; granting to any corporation, association, or individual any special or exclusive privilege or immunity, or to any corporation, association, or individual the right to lay down a railroad track; nor shall the General Assembly indirectly enact such special or local law by the partial repeal of a general law; but laws repealing local or special acts may be passed; nor shall any law be passed granting powers or privileges in any case where the granting of such powers and privileges shall have been provided for by general law, nor where the courts have jurisdiction to grant the same or give the relief asked for.

SEC. 8. No local or special bill shall be passed unless notice of the intention to apply therefor shall have been published in the locality where the matter or the thing to be effected may be situated, which notice shall be at least thirty days prior to the introduction into the General Assembly of such bill and in the manner to be provided by law; the evidence of such notice having been published shall be exhibited in the General Assembly before such act shall be passed.

SEC. 9. The presiding officer of each house shall, in the presence of the house over which he presides, sign all bills and joint resolution passed by the General Assembly, after their titles have been publicly read immediately before signing; and the fact of signing shall be entered on the journal.

SEC. 10. The General Assembly shall prescribe by law the number, duties and compensation of the officers and employés of each house, and no payment shall be made from the State treasury, or be in any way authorized, to any person, except to an acting officer or employé elected or appointed in pursuance of law.

SEC. 11. No bill shall be passed giving any extra compensation to any public officer, servant, employé, agent or contractor, after services shall have been rendered or contract made, nor providing for the payment of any claim against the Commonwealth without previous authority of law.

SEC. 12. All stationery, printing paper, and fuel used in the legislative and other departments of government shall be furnished, and the printing, binding, and distributing of the laws, journals, department reports, and all other printing and binding and the repairing and furnishing the halls and rooms used for the meeting of the General Assembly and its committees, shall be performed under contract to be given to the lowest responsible bidder below such maximum price and under such regulations as shall be prescribed by law: no member or officer of any department of the government shall be in any way interested in such contracts, and all such contracts shall be subject to the approval of the Governor, auditor-general, and State treasurer.

SEC. 13. No law shall extend the term of any public officer, or increase or diminish his salary or emoluments, after his election or appointment.

SEC. 14. All bills for raising revenue shall originate in in the House of Representatives, but the Senate may propose amendments as in other bills.

SEC. 15. The general appropriation bill shall embrace nothing but appropriations for the ordinary expenses of the executive, legislative, and judicial departments of the Commonwealth, interest on the public debt, and for public schools; all other appropriations shall be made by separate bills, each embracing but one subject.

SEC. 16. No money shall be paid out of the treasury except upon appropriations made by law, and on warrant drawn by the proper officer in pursuance thereof.

SEC. 17. No appropriation shall be made to any charitable or educational institution not under the absolute control of the Commonwealth, other than normal schools established by law for the professional training of teachers for the public schools of the State, except by a vote of two thirds of all the members elected to each house.

SEC. 18. No appropriations except for pensions or gratuities for military services, shall be made for charitable, educational or benevolent purposes to any person or community, nor to any denominational or sectarian institution, corporation, or association.

SEC. 19. The General Assembly may make appropriations of money to institutions wherein the widows of soldiers are supported or assisted, or the orphans of soldiers are maintained and educated, but such appropriations shall be applied exclusively to the support of such widows and orphans.

SEC. 20. The General Assembly shall not delegate to any special commission, private corporation or association, any power to make, supervise, or interfere with any municipal improvement, money, property or effects, whether held in trust, or otherwise, or to levy taxes or perform any municipal function whatever.

SEC. 21. No act of the General Assembly shall

limit the amount to be recovered for injuries resulting in death, or for injuries to persons or property: and in case of death from such injuries the right of action shall survive, and the General Assembly shall prescribe for whose benefit such actions shall be prosecuted. No act shall prescribe any limitations of time within which suits may be brought against corporations for injuries to persons or property, or for other causes different from those fixed by general laws regulating actions against natural persons, and such acts now existing are avoided.

SEC. 22. No act of the General Assembly shall authorize the investment of trust funds by executors, administrators, guardians or other trustees, in the bonds or stock of any private corporation, and such acts now existing are avoided, saving investments heretofore made.

SEC. 23. The power to change the venue in civil and criminal cases shall be vested in the courts, to be exercised in such manner as shall be provided by law.

SEC. 24. No obligation or liability of any railroad or other corporation, held or owned by the Commonwealth, shall ever be exchanged, transferred, remitted, postponed, or in any way diminished by the General Assembly, nor shall such liability or obligation be released, except by payment thereof into the State treasury.

SEC. 25. When the General Assembly shall be convened in special session there shall be no legislation upon subjects other than those designated in the proclamation of the Governor calling such session.

SEC. 26. Every order, resolution, or vote, to which the concurrence of both houses may be necessary (except on the question of adjournment), shall be presented to the Governor, and, before it shall take effect, be approved by him, or, being disapproved, shall be re-passed by two thirds of both houses, according to the rules and limitations prescribed in case of a bill.

SEC. 27. No State office shall be continued or created for the inspection or measuring of any merchandise, manufacture, or commodity, but any county or municipality may appoint such officers when authorized by law.

SEC. 28. No law changing the location of the capital of the State shall be valid, until the same shall have been submitted to the qualified electors of the Commonwealth, at a general election, and ratified and approved by them.

SEC. 29. A member of the General Assembly who shall solicit, demand, or receive or consent to receive, directly or indirectly, for himself or for another, from any company, corporation or person, any money, office, appointment, employment, testimonial, reward, thing of value, or enjoyment, or of personal advantage, or promise thereof, for his vote, or official influence, or for withholding the same, or with an understanding, expressed or implied, that his vote or official action shall be, in any way, influenced thereby, or who shall solicit, or demand any such money, or other advantage, matter, or thing aforesaid for another, as the consideration of his vote or official influence, or for withholding the same, or shall give, or withhold his vote or influence, in consideration of the payment or promise of such money, advantage, matter or thing to another, shall be held guilty of bribery within the meaning of this Constitution, and shall incur the disabilities provided thereby for said offense, and such additional punishment as is or shall be provided by law.

Sec. 30. Any person who shall, directly or indirectly, offer, give, or promise, any money, or thing of value, testimonial, privilege or personal advantage, to any executive or judicial officer, or member of the General Assembly, to influence him in the performance of any of his public or official duties, shall be guilty of bribery, and be punished in such manner as shall be provided by law.

Sec. 31. The offense of corrupt solicitation of members of the General Assembly, or of public officers of the State, or of any municipal division thereof, and any occupation, or practice of solicitation, of such members or officers, to influence their official action, shall be defined by law, and shall be punished by fine and imprisonment.

Sec. 32. Any person may be compelled to testify in any lawful investigation, or judicial proceeding, against any person, who may be charged with having committed the offense of bribery or corrupt solicitation, or practices of solicitation, and shall not be permitted to withhold his testimony upon the ground that it may criminate himself, or subject him to public infamy; but such testimony shall not afterwards be used against him in any judicial proceeding, except for perjury in giving such testimony; and any person convicted of either' of the offenses aforesaid shall, as part of the punishment therefor, be disqualified from holding any office or position of honor, trust, or profit in this Commonwealth.

Sec. 33. A member who has a personal or private interest in any measure or bill proposed or pending before the General Assembly, shall disclose the fact to the house of which he is a member, and shall not vote thereon.

Article IV.

The Executive.

SEC. 1. The executive department of this Commonwealth shall consist of a Governor, Lieutenant-Governor, Secretary of the Commonwealth, Attorney General, Auditor General, State Treasurer, Secretary of Internal Affairs, and a Superintendent of Public Instruction.

SEC. 2. The supreme executive power shall be vested in the Governor, who shall take care that the laws be faithfully executed; he shall be chosen on the day of the general election, by the qualified electors of the Commonwealth, at the places where they shall vote for representatives. The returns of every election for Governor shall be sealed up and transmitted to the seat of government, directed to the president of the Senate, who shall open and publish them in the presence of the members of both houses of the General Assembly. The person having the highest number of votes shall be Governor; but if two or more be equal and highest in votes, one of them shall be chosen Governor by the joint vote of the members of both houses. Contested elections shall be determined by a committee, to be selected from both houses of the General Assembly, and formed and regulated in such manner as shall be directed by law.

SEC. 3. The Governor shall hold his office during four years, from the third Tuesday of January next ensuing his election, and shall not be eligible to the office for the next succeeding term.

SEC. 4. A Lieutenant-Governor shall be chosen at the same time, in the same manner, for the same term, and subject to the same provisions as the Governor; he shall be president of the Senate, but shall have no vote unless they be equally divided.

SEC. 5. No person shall be eligible to the office of Governor or Lieutenant-Governor, except a citizen of the United States, who shall have attained the age of thirty years, and have been seven years next preceding his election an inhabitant of the State, unless he shall have been absent on the public business of the United States or of this State.

SEC. 6. No member of Congress, or person holding any office under the United States, or this State, shall exercise the office of Governor or Lieutenant-Governor.

SEC. 7. The Governor shall be commander-in-chief of the army and navy of the Commonwealth, and of the militia, except when they shall be called into the actual service of the United States.

SEC. 8. He shall nominate, and, by and with the advice and consent of two thirds of all the members of the Senate, appoint a secretary of the Commonwealth and an attorney general during pleasure, a superintendent of public instruction for four years, and such other officers of the Commonwealth as he is or may be authorized by the Constitution or by law to appoint; he shall have power to fill all vacancies that may happen in offices to which he may appoint, during the recess of the Senate, by granting commissions which shall expire at the end of their next session; he shall have power to fill any vacancy that may happen, during the recess of the Senate, in the office of auditor general, State treasurer, secretary of internal affairs, or superintendent of public instruction, in a judicial office, or in any other elective office which he is or may be authorized to fill; if the vacancy shall happen during the session of the Senate, the Governor shall nominate to the Senate, before their final adjournment, a proper person to fill said vacancy; but in any such case of vacancy, in an elective office, a person shall be chosen to said office at the next general election, unless the vacancy shall happen within three calendar months immediately preceding such election, in which case the election for said office shall be at the second succeeding general election. In acting on executive nominations the Senate shall sit with open doors, and, in confirming or rejecting the nominations of the Governor, the vote shall be taken by yeas and nays, and shall be entered on the journal.

SEC. 9. He shall have power to remit fines and forfeitures, to grant reprieves, commutations of sentences and pardons, except in cases of impeachment; but no pardon shall be granted nor sentence commuted, except upon the recommendation, in writing, of the Lieutenant-Governor, secretary of the Commonwealth, attorney general, and secretary of internal affairs, or any three of them, after full hearing, upon due public notice and in open session; and such recommendation, with the reasons therefor at length, shall be recorded and filed in the office of the secretary of the Commonwealth.

SEC. 10. He may require information, in writing, from the officers of the executive department, upon any subject relating to the duties of their respective offices.

SEC. 11. He shall, from time to time, give to the General Assembly information of the state of the Commonwealth, and recommend to their consideration such measures as he may judge expedient.

SEC. 12. He may on extraordinary occasions, convene the General Assembly; and in case of disagreement between the two houses, with respect to the time of adjournment, adjourn them to such time as he shall think proper, not exceeding four months. He shall have power to convene the Senate in extraordinary session by proclamation, for the transaction of executive business.

SEC. 13. In case of the death, conviction or impeachment, failure to qualify, resignation, or other disability of the Governor, the powers, duties and emoluments of the office, for the remainder of the term, or until the disability be removed, shall devolve upon the Lieutenant-Governor.

SEC. 14. In case of a vacancy in the office of Lieutenant-Governor, or when the Lieutenant-Governor shall be impeached by the House of Representatives, or shall be unable to exercise the duties of his office, the powers, duties and emoluments thereof for the remainder of the term, or until the disability be removed, shall devolve upon the president *pro tempore* of the Senate; and the president *pro tempore* of the Senate shall in like manner become Governor if a vacancy or disability shall occur in the office of Governor; his seat as senator shall become vacant whenever he shall become Governor, and shall be filled by election as any other vacancy in the Senate.

SEC. 15. Every bill which shall have passed both houses shall be presented to the Governor; if he approve he shall sign it; but if he shall not approve he shall return it, with his objections to the house in which it shall have originated, which house shall enter the objections at large upon their journal and proceed to reconsider it. If, after such reconsideration, two thirds of all the members elected to that house shall agree to pass the bill, it shall be sent with the objections, to the other house, by which likewise it shall be reconsidered, and if approved by two thirds of all the members elected to that house, it shall be a law; but in such cases the votes of both houses shall be determined by yeas and nays and the names of the members voting for and against the bill shall be entered on the journals of each house respectively. If any bill shall not be returned by the Governor within ten days after it shall have been presented to him, the same shall be a law, in like manner as if he had signed it, unless the General Assembly, by their adjournment prevent its return; in which case it shall be a law, unless he shall file the same with his objections, in the office of the secretary of the Commonwealth, and give notice thereof by public proclamation within thirty days after such adjournment.

SEC. 16. The Governor shall have power to disapprove of any item or items of any bill making appropriations of money, embracing distinct items, and the part or parts of the bill approved shall be the law, and the item or items of appropriations disapproved shall be void, unless re-passed according to the rules and limitations prescribed for the passage of other bills over the executive veto.

SEC. 17. The Chief Justice of the Supreme Court shall preside upon the trial of any contested election of Governor or Lieutenant-Governor, and shall decide questions regarding the admissibility of evidence, and shall, upon request of the committee, pronounce his opinion upon other questions of law involved in the trial. The Governor and Lieutenant-Governor shall exercise the duties of their respective offices until their successor shall be duly qualified.

SEC. 18. the secretary of the Commonwealth shall keep a record of all official acts and proceedings of the Governor, and when required, lay the same, with all papers, minutes and vouchers relating thereto, before either branch of the General Assembly, and perform such other duties as may be enjoined upon him by law.

SEC. 19. The secretary of internal affairs shall exercise all the powers, and perform all the duties of the surveyor general, subject to such changes as shall be made by law. His department shall embrace a bureau of industrial statistics, and he shall discharge such duties relating to corporations, to the charitable institutions, the agricultural, manufacturing, mining, mineral, timber and other material or business interests of the State as may be prescribed by law. He shall annually, and at such other times as may be required by law, make report to the General Assembly.

SEC. 20. The superintendent of public instruction shall exercise all the powers and perform all the duties of the superintendent of common schools, subject to such changes as shall be made by law.

SEC. 21. The term of the secretary of internal affairs shall be four years; of the auditor general three years, and of the State treasurer two years. These officers shall be chosen by the qualified electors of the State at general elections. No person elected to the office of auditor general or State treasurer shall be capable of holding the same office for two consecutive terms.

SEC. 22. The present great seal of Pennsylvania shall be the seal of the State. All commissions shall be in the name and by authority of the Commonwealth of Pennsylvania, and be sealed with the State seal, and signed by the Governor.

ARTICLE V.

THE JUDICIARY.

SEC. 1. The judicial power of this Commonwealth shall be vested in a Supreme Court, in courts of common pleas, courts of oyer and terminer and general jail delivery, courts of quarter sessions of the peace, orphans' courts, magistrates' courts, and in such other courts as the General Assembly may from time to time establish.

SEC. 2. The Supreme Court shall consist of seven judges, who shall be elected by the qualified electors of the State at large. They shall hold their offices for the term of twenty-one years, if they so long behave themselves well, but shall not be again eligible. The judge whose commission shall first expire shall be Chief Justice, and thereafter each judge whose commission shall first expire shall in turn be Chief Justice.

SEC. 3. The jurisdiction of the Supreme Court shall extend over the State, and the judges thereof shall, by virtue of their offices, be justices of oyer and terminer and general jail delivery in the several counties; they shall have original jurisdiction in cases of injunction where a corporation is a party defendant, of *habeas corpus*, of *mandamus* to courts of inferior jurisdiction, and of *quo warranto* as to all officers of the Commonwealth whose jurisdiction extends over the State, but shall not exercise any other original jurisdiction; they shall have appellate jurisdiction by appeal, *certiorari*, or writ of error in all cases, as is now or may hereafter be provided by law.

SEC. 4. Until otherwise directed by law, the courts of common pleas shall continue as at present established, except as herein changed; not more than four counties shall, at any time, be included in one judicial district organized for said courts.

SEC. 5. Whenever a county shall contain forty thousand inhabitants it shall constitute a separate judicial district, and shall elect one judge learned in the law; and the General Assembly shall provide for additional judges, as the business of the said districts may require. Counties containing a population less than is sufficient to constitute separate districts shall be formed into convenient single districts, or, if necessary, may be attached to contiguous districts as the General Assembly may provide. The office of associate judge, not learned in the law, is abolished in counties forming separate districts; but the several associate judges in office when this Constitution shall be adopted shall serve for their unexpired terms.

. . . .

SEC. 9. Judges of the courts of common pleas learned in the law shall be judges of the courts of oyer and terminer, quarter sessions of the peace, and general jail delivery, and of the orphans' court, and within their respective districts, shall be justices of the peace as to criminal matters.

SEC. 10. The judges of the courts of common pleas, within their respective counties shall have power to issue writs of *certiorari* to justices of the peace, and other inferior courts, not of record, and to cause their proceedings to be brought before them, and right and justice to be done.

SEC. 11. Except as otherwise provided in this Constitution, justices of the peace, or aldermen, shall be elected in the several wards, districts, boroughs, and townships at the time of the election of constables by the qualified electors thereof, in such manner as shall be directed by law, and shall be commissioned by the Governor for a term of five years. No township, ward, district, or borough shall elect more than two justices of the peace, or aldermen, without the consent of a majority of the qualified electors within such township, ward, or borough; no person shall be elected to such office unless he shall have resided within the township, borough, ward, or district for one year next preceding his election. In cities containing over fifty thousand inhabitants not more than one alderman shall be elected in each ward or district.

. . . .

SEC. 14. In all cases of summary conviction in this Commonwealth, or of judgment in suit for a penalty before a magistrate or court not of record, either party may appeal to such court of record, as may be prescribed by law, upon allowance of the appellate court, or judge thereof, upon cause shown.

SEC. 15. All judges required to be learned in the law, except the judges of the Supreme Court, shall be elected by the qualified electors of the respective districts over which they are to preside, and shall hold their offices for the period of ten years, if they shall so long behave themselves well; but for any reasonable cause, which shall not be sufficient ground for impeachment, the Governor may remove any of them on the address of two thirds of each house of the General Assembly.

SEC. 16. Whenever two judges of the Supreme Court are to be chosen for the same term of service, each voter shall vote for one only, and when three are to be chosen he shall vote for no more than two; candidates highest in vote shall be declared elected.

SEC. 17. Should any two or more judges of the Supreme Court, or any two or more judges of the court of common pleas for the same district, be elected at the same time, they shall, as soon after the election as convenient, cast lots for priority of commission, and certify the result to the Governor, who shall issue their commissions in accordance therewith.

SEC. 18. The judges of the Supreme Court and the judges of the several courts of common pleas, and all other judges required to be learned in the law, shall, at stated times, receive for their services an adequate compensation, which shall be fixed by law, and paid by the State. They shall receive no other compensation, fees, or perquisites of office for their services from any source, nor hold any other office of profit under the United States, this State, or any other State.

SEC. 19. The judges of the Supreme Court, during their continuance in office, shall reside within this Commonwealth, and the other judges during their continuance in office shall reside within the districts for which they shall be respectively elected.

SEC. 20. The several courts of common pleas, besides the powers herein conferred, shall have and exercise within their respective districts, subject to such changes as may be made by law, such chancery powers as are now vested by law in the several courts of common pleas of this Commonwealth, or as may hereafter be conferred upon them by law.

SEC. 21. No duties shall be imposed by law upon the Supreme Court or any of the judges thereof except such as are judicial, nor shall any of the judges exercise any power of appointment except as herein provided. The court of *nisi prius* is hereby abolished, and no court of original jurisdiction to be presided over by any one or more of the judges of the Supreme Court shall be established.

SEC. 22. In every county wherein the population shall exceed one hundred and fifty thousand, the General Assembly shall, and in any other county may, establish a separate orphans' court, to consist of one or more judges who shall be learned in the law, which court shall exercise all the jurisdiction and powers now vested in or which may hereafter be conferred upon the orphans' courts, and thereupon the jurisdiction of the judges of the court of common pleas within such county, in orphans' court proceedings, shall cease and determine. In any county in which a separate orphans' court shall be established, the register of wills shall be clerk of such court and subject to its directions, in all matters pertaining to his office; he may appoint assistant clerks, but only with the consent and approval of said court. All accounts filed with him as register or as clerk of the said separate orphans' court, shall be audited by the court without expense to parties, except where all parties in interest in a pending proceeding shall nominate an auditor whom the court may, in its discretion, appoint. In every county orphans' courts shall possess all the powers and jurisdiction of a registers' court, and separate registers' courts are hereby abolished.

SEC. 23. The style of all process shall be "The Commonwealth of Pennsylvania." All prosecutions shall be carried on in the name and by the authority of the Commonwealth of Pennsylvania, and conclude "against the peace and dignity of the same."

SEC. 24. In all cases of felonious homicide, and in such other criminal cases as may be provided for by law, the accused, after conviction and sentence, may remove the indictment, record, and all proceedings to the Supreme Court for review.

SEC. 25. Any vacancy happening by death, resignation, or otherwise, in any court of record, shall be filled by appointment by the Governor, to continue till the first Monday of January next succeeding the first general election, which shall occur three or more months after the happening of such vacancy.

SEC. 26. All laws relating to courts shall be general, and of uniform operations, and the organization, jurisdiction, and powers of all courts of the same class or grade, so far as regulated by law, and the force and effect of the process and judgments of such courts shall be uniform; and the General Assembly is hereby prohibited from creating other courts to exercise the powers vested by this Constitution in the judges of the courts of common pleas and orphans' courts.

SEC. 27. The parties by agreement filed, may in any civil case dispense with trial by jury, and submit the decision of such case to the court having jurisdiction thereof, and such court shall hear and determine the same; and the judgment thereon shall be subject to writ of error, as in other cases.

ARTICLE VI.

IMPEACHMENT AND REMOVAL FROM OFFICE.

SEC. 1. The House of Representatives shall have the sole power of impeachment.

SEC. 2. All impeachments shall be tried by the Senate. When sitting for that purpose, the senators shall be upon oath or affirmation. No person shall be convicted without the concurrence of two thirds of the members present.

SEC. 3. The Governor, and all other civil officers, shall be liable to impeachment for any misdemeanor in office; but judgment in such cases shall not extend further than to removal from office, and disqualification to hold any office of trust or profit under this Commonwealth; the person accused, whether convicted or acquitted, shall nevertheless be liable to indictment, trial, judgment, and punishment, according to law.

SEC. 4. All officers shall hold their offices on the condition that they behave themselves well while in office, and shall be removed on conviction of misbehavior in office, or of any infamous crime. Appointed officers, other than judges of the courts of record and the superintendent of public instruction, may be removed at the pleasure of the power by which they shall have been appointed. All officers elected by the people, except Governor, Lieutenant Governor, members of the General Assembly, and judges of the courts of record learned in the law, shall be removed by the Governor for reasonable cause, after due notice and full hearing, on the address of two thirds of the Senate.

ARTICLE VII.

OATH OF OFFICE.

SEC. 1. Senators and representatives, and all judicial, State, and county officers, shall, before entering on the duties of their respective offices, take and subscribe the following oath or affirmation:

"I do solemnly swear (or affirm) that I will support, obey, and defend the Constitution of the United States, and the Constitution of this Commonwealth, and that I will discharge the duties of my office with fidelity; that I have not paid or contributed, or promised to pay or contribute, either directly or indirectly, any money or other valuable thing, to procure my nomination or election (or appointment), except for necessary and proper expenses expressly authorized by law; that I have not knowingly violated any election law of this Commonwealth, or procured it to be done by others in my behalf; that I will not knowingly receive, directly or indirectly, any moneys or other valuable thing for the performance or non-performance of any act or duty pertaining to my office, other than the compensation allowed by law."

The foregoing oath shall be administered by some person authorized to administer oaths, and in the case of State officers and judges of the Supreme Court, shall be filed in the office of the secretary of the Commonwealth, and in the case of other judicial and county officers, in the office of the prothonotary of the county in which the same is taken; any person refusing to take said oath or affirmation shall forfeit his office, and any person who shall be convicted of having sworn or affirmed falsely, or of having violated said oath or affirmation, shall be guilty of perjury, and be forever disqualified from holding any office of trust or profit within this Commonwealth. The oath to the members of the Senate and House of Representatives shall be administered by one of the judges of the Supreme Court or of a court of common pleas, learned in the law, in the hall of the house to which the members shall be elected.

ARTICLE VIII.

SUFFRAGE AND ELECTIONS.

SEC. 1. Every male citizen twenty-one years of age possessing the following qualifications shall be entitled to vote at all elections: *First*. He shall have been a citizen of the United States at least one month. *Second*. He shall have resided in the State one year (or if, having previously been a qualified elector or native born citizen of the State, he shall have removed therefrom and returned, then six months) immediately preceding the election. *Third*. He shall have resided in the election district where he shall offer to vote at least two months immediately preceding the election. *Fourth*. If twenty-two years of age or upwards he shall have paid within two years a State or county tax, which shall have been assessed at least two months and paid at least one month before the election.

SEC. 2. The general election shall be held annually on the Tuesday next following the first Monday of November, but the General Assembly may by law fix a different day, two thirds of all the members of each house consenting thereto.

SEC. 3. All elections for city, ward, borough, and township officers, for regular terms of service, shall be held on the third Tuesday of February.

SEC. 4. All elections by the citizens shall be by ballot. Every ballot voted shall be numbered in the order in which it shall be received, and the number recorded by the election officers on the list of voters, opposite the name of the elector who presents the ballot. Any elector may write his name upon his ticket, or cause the same to be written thereon and attested by a citizen of the district. The election officers shall be sworn or affirmed not to disclose how any elector shall have voted unless required to do so as witnesses in a judicial proceeding.

SEC. 5. Electors shall in all cases, except treason, felony, and breach or surety of the peace, be privileged from arrest during their attendance on elections, and going to and returning therefrom.

SEC. 6. Whenever any of the qualified electors of this Commonwealth shall be in actual military service, under a requisition from the President of the United States, or by the authority of this Commonwealth, such electors may exercise the right of suffrage in all elections by the citizens, under such regulations as are, or shall be, prescribed by law, as fully as if they were present at their usual places of election.

SEC. 7. All laws regulating the holding of elections by the citizens or for the registration of electors shall be uniform throughout the State, but no elector shall be deprived of the privilege of voting by reason of his name not being registered.

SEC. 8. Any person who shall give, or promise or offer to give, to an elector, any money, reward or other valuable consideration for his vote at an election, or for withholding the same, or who shall give or promise to give such consideration to any other person or party for such elector's vote or for the withholding thereof, and any elector who shall receive or agree to receive, for himself or for another, any money, reward or other valuable consideration for his vote at an election, or for withholding the same, shall thereby forfeit the right to vote at such election, and any elector whose right to vote shall be challenged for such cause before the election officers, shall be required to swear or affirm that the matter of the challenge is untrue before his vote shall be received.

SEC. 9. Any person who shall, while a candidate for office, be guilty of bribery, fraud or wilful violation of any election law, shall be forever disqualified from holding an office of trust or profit in this Commonwealth; and any person convicted of wilful violation of the election laws shall, in addition to any penalties provided by law, be deprived of the right of suffrage absolutely for a term of four years.

SEC. 10. In trials of contested elections and in proceedings for the investigation of elections, no person shall be permitted to withhold his testimony upon the ground that it may criminate himself or subject him to public infamy; but such testimony shall not afterwards be used against him in any judicial proceeding except for perjury in giving such testimony.

SEC. 11. Townships and wards of cities or boroughs, shall form or be divided into election districts of compact and contiguous territory, in such manner as the court of quarter sessions of the city or county in which the same are located may direct; but districts in cities of over one hundred thousand inhabitants shall be divided by the courts of quarter sessions, having jurisdiction therein, whenever at the next preceding election more than two hundred and fifty votes shall have been polled therein ; and other election districts whenever the court of the proper county shall be of opinion that the convenience of the electors and the public interests will be promoted thereby.

SEC. 12. All elections by persons in a representative capacity shall be *viva voce.*

SEC. 13. For the purpose of voting no person shall be deemed to have gained a residence by reason of his presence, or lost it by reason of his absence, while employed in the service, either civil or military, of this State or of the United States, nor while engaged in the navigation of the waters of the State or of the United States, or on the high seas, nor while a student of any institution of learning, nor while kept in any poor-house or other asylum at public expense, nor while confined in public prison.

SEC. 14. District election boards shall consist of a judge and two inspectors, who shall be chosen annually by the citizens. Each elector shall have the right to vote for the judge and one inspector, and each inspector shall appoint one clerk. The first election board for any new district shall be selected, and vacancies in election boards filled as shall be provided by law. Election officers shall be privileged from arrest upon days of election, and while engaged in making up and transmitting returns, except upon warrant of court of record, or judge thereof, for an election fraud, for felony, or for wanton breach of the peace. In cities they may claim exemption from jury duty during their terms of service.

SEC. 15. No person shall be qualified to serve as

an election officer who shall hold, or shall within two months have held, an office, appointment, or employment in or under the government of the United States or of this State, or of any city or county, or of any municipal board, commission, or trust in any city, save only justices of the peace, and aldermen, notaries public, and persons in the militia service of the State; nor shall any election officer be eligible to any civil office to be filled at an election at which he shall serve, save only to such subordinate municipal or local officers, below the grade of city or county officers, as shall be designated by general law.

SEC. 16. The courts of common pleas of the several counties of the Commonwealth shall have power, within their respective jurisdictions, to appoint overseers of election to supervise the proceedings of election officers, and to make report to the court as may be required; such appointments to be made for any district in a city or county upon petition of five citizens, lawful voters of such election districts, setting forth that such appointment is a reasonable precaution to secure the purity and fairness of elections; overseers shall be two in number for an election district, shall be residents therein, and shall be persons qualified to serve upon election boards, and in each case members of different political parties. Whenever the members of an election board shall differ in opinion, the overseers, if they shall be agreed thereon, shall decide the question of difference; in appointing overseers of election, all the law judges of the proper court, able to act at the time, shall concur in the appointments made.

SEC. 17. The trial and determination of contested elections of electors of President and Vice-President, members of the General Assembly, and of all public officers, whether State, judicial, municipal, or local, shall be by the courts of law, or by one or more of the law judges thereof, the General Assembly shall, by general law, designate the courts and judges by whom the several classes of election contests shall be tried, and regulate the manner of trial, and all matters incident thereto; but no such law assigning jurisdiction, or regulating its exercise, shall apply to any contest arising out of an election held before its passage.

Article IX.

Taxation and Finance.

Sec. 1. All taxes shall be uniform, upon the same class of subjects, within the territorial limits of the authority levying the tax, and shall be levied and collected under general laws; but the General Assembly may, by general laws, exempt from taxation public property used for public purposes, actual places of religious worship, places of burial not used or held for private or corporate profit, and institutions of a purely public charity.

Sec. 2. All laws exempting property from taxation, other than the property above enumerated, shall be void.

Sec. 3. The power to tax corporations and corporate property shall not be surrendered or suspended by any contract or grant to which the State shall be a party.

Sec. 4. No debt shall be created by or on behalf of the State, except to supply casual deficiencies of revenue, repel invasions, suppress insurrection, defend the State in war, or to pay existing debt; and the debt created to supply deficiencies in revenue shall never exceed, in the aggregate at any one time, one million of dollars.

SEC. 5. All laws authorizing the borrowing of money by and on behalf of the State, shall specify the purpose for which the money is to be used, and the money so borrowed shall be used for the purpose specified, and no other.

SEC. 6. The credit of the Commonwealth shall not be pledged or loaned to any individual, company, corporation or association, nor shall the Commonwealth become a joint-owner or stockholder in any company, association or corporation.

SEC. 7. The General Assembly shall not authorize any county, city, borough, township or incorporated district to become a stockholder in any company, association or corporation, or to obtain or appropriate money for, or to loan its credit to, any corporation, association, institution or individual.

SEC. 8. The debt of any county, city, borough, township, school district or other municipality or incorporated district, except as herein provided, shall never exceed seven per centum upon the assessed value of the taxable property therein, nor shall any such municipality or district incur any new debt, or increase its indebtedness to an amount exceeding two per centum upon such assessed valuation of property, without the assent of the electors thereof at a public election in such manner as shall be provided by law; but any city, the debt of which now exceeds seven per centum of such assessed valuation, may be authorized by law to increase the same three per centum, in the aggregate at any one time, upon such valuation.

SEC. 9. The Commonwealth shall not assume the debt, or any part thereof, of any city, county, borough or township, unless such debt shall have been contracted to enable the State to repel invasion, suppress domestic insurrection, defend itself in time of war, or to assist the State in the discharge of any portion of its present indebtedness.

SEC. 10. Any county, township, school district or other municipality, incurring any indebtedness, shall, at or before the time of so doing, provide for the collection of an annual tax, sufficient to pay the interest, and also the principal thereof within thirty years.

SEC. 11. To provide for the payment of the present State debt, and any additional debt contracted as aforesaid, the General Assembly shall continue and maintain the sinking fund sufficient to pay the accruing interest on such debt, and annually to reduce the principal thereof by a sum not less than two hundred and fifty thousand dollars ; the said sinking fund shall consist of the proceeds of the sales of the public works, or any part thereof, and of the income or proceeds of the sale of any stocks owned by the Commonwealth, together with other funds and resources that may be designated by law, and shall be increased from time to time by assigning to it any part of the taxes, or other revenues of the State, not required for the ordinary and current expenses of government ; and unless in case of war, invasion or insurrection, no part of the said sinking fund shall be used or applied otherwise than in the extinguishment of the public debt.

SEC. 12. The moneys of the State, over and above the necessary reserve, shall be used in the payment of the debt of the State, either directly or through the sinking fund, and the moneys of the sinking fund shall never be invested in or loaned upon the security of anything, except the bonds of the United States, or of this State.

SEC. 13. The moneys held as necessary reserve shall be limited by law to the amount required for current expenses, and shall be secured and kept as may be provided by law. Monthly statements shall be published, showing the amount of such moneys, where the same are deposited and how secured.

SEC. 14. The making of profit out of the public moneys, or using the same for any purpose not authorized by law, by any officer of the State, or member or officer of the General Assembly, shall be a misdemeanor, and shall be punished as may be provided by law, but part of such punishment shall be disqualification to hold office for a period of not less than five years.

ARTICLE X.

EDUCATION.

SEC. 1. The General Assembly shall provide for the maintenance and support of a thorough and efficient system of public schools, wherein all the children of this Commonwealth, above the age of six years, may be educated, and shall appropriate at least one million dollars each year for that purpose.

SEC. 2. No money raised for the support of the public schools of the Commonwealth, shall be appropriated to, or used for the support of any sectarian school.

SEC. 3. Women twenty-one years of age and upwards shall be eligible to any office of control or management under the school laws of this State,

ARTICLE XI.

MILITIA.

SEC. 1. The freemen of this Commonwealth shall be armed, organized, and disciplined for its defense, when, and in such manner as may be directed by law. The General Assembly shall provide for maintaining the militia, by appropriations from the treasury of the Commonwealth, and may exempt from military service persons having conscientious scruples against bearing arms.

ARTICLE XII.
PUBLIC OFFICERS.

SEC. 1. All officers whose selection is not provided for in this Constitution, shall be elected or appointed, as may be directed by law.

SEC. 2. No member of Congress from this State, nor any person holding or exercising any office or appointment of trust or profit under the United States, shall at the same time hold or exercise any office in this State to which a salary, fees or perquisites shall be attached. The General Assembly may by law declare what offices are incompatible.

SEC. 3. Any person who shall fight a duel, or send a challenge for that purpose, or be aider or abettor in fighting a duel, shall be deprived of the right of holding any office of honor or profit in this State, and may be otherwise punished as shall be prescribed by law.

ARTICLE XIII.
NEW COUNTIES.

SEC. 1. No new county shall be established which shall reduce any county to less than four hundred square miles, or to less than twenty thousand inhabitants, nor shall any county be formed of less area, or containing a less population; nor shall any line thereof pass within ten miles of the county seat of any county proposed to be divided.

ARTICLE XIV.
COUNTY OFFICERS.

SEC. 1. County officers shall consist of sheriffs, coroners, prothonotaries, registers of wills, recorder of deeds, commissioners, treasurers, surveyors, auditors or controllers, clerks of the courts, district attorneys, and such others as may from time to time be established by law; and no sheriff or treasurer shall be eligible for the term next succeeding the one for which he may be elected.

SEC. 2. County officers shall be elected at the general elections, and shall hold their offices for the term of three years beginning on the first Monday of January next after their election, and until their successors shall be duly qualified; all vacancies not otherwise provided for, shall be filled in such manner as may be provided by law.

SEC. 3. No person shall be appointed to any office within any county, who shall not have been a citizen and an inhabitant therein one year next before his appointment, if the county shall have been so long erected, but if it shall not have been so long erected, then within the limits of the county or counties out of which it shall have been taken.

SEC. 4. Prothonotaries, clerks of the courts, recorders of deeds, registers of wills, county surveyors, and sheriffs, shall keep their offices in the county town of the county in which they respectively shall be officers.

SEC. 5. The compensation of county officers shall be regulated by law, and all county officers who are or may be salaried shall pay all fees which they may be authorized to receive, into the treasury of the county or State, as may be directed by law. In counties containing over one hundred and fifty thousand inhabitants all county officers shall be paid by salary, and the salary of any such officer and his clerks, heretofore paid by fees, shall not exceed the aggregate amount of fees earned during his term and collected by or for him.

SEC. 6. The General Assembly shall provide by law for the strict accountability of all county, township, and borough officers, as well as for the fees which may be collected by them, as for all public or municipal moneys which may be paid to them.

SEC. 7. Three county commissioners and three county auditors shall be elected in each county where such officers are chosen, in the year one thousand eight hundred and seventy-five and every third year thereafter; and in the election of said officers, each qualified elector shall vote for no more than two persons, and the three persons having the highest number of votes shall be elected; any casual vacancy in the office of county commissioner or county auditor shall be filled by the court of common pleas of the county in which such vacancy shall occur, by the appointment of an elector of the proper county who shall have voted for the commissioner or auditor whose place is to be filled.

· ARTICLE XV.

CITIES AND CITY CHARTERS.

SEC. 1. Cities may be chartered whenever a majority of the electors of any town or borough having a population of at least ten thousand shall vote at any general election in favor of the same.

SEC. 2. No debt shall be contracted or liability incurred by any municipal commission, except in pursuance of an appropriation previously made therefor by the municipal government.

SEC. 3. Every city shall create a sinking fund, which shall be inviolably pledged for the payment of its funded debt.

ARTICLE XVI.

PRIVATE CORPORATIONS.

SEC. 1. All existing charters, or grants of special

or exclusive privileges, under which a *bona fide* organization shall not have taken place and business been commenced in good faith, at the time of the adoption of this Constitution, shall thereafter have no validity.

SEC. 2. The General Assembly shall not remit the forfeiture of the charter of any corporation now existing, or alter or amend the same, or pass any other general or special law for the benefit of such corporation, except upon the condition that such corporation shall thereafter hold its charter subject to the provisions of this Constitution.

SEC. 3. The exercise of the right of eminent domain shall never be abridged or so construed as to prevent the General Assembly from taking the property and franchises of incorporated companies, and subjecting them to public use, the same as the property of individuals; and the exercise of the police power of the State shall never be abridged or so construed as to permit corporations to conduct their business in such manner as to infringe the equal rights of individuals or the general well-being of the State.

SEC. 4. In all elections for directors or managers of a corporation each member or shareholder may cast the whole number of his votes for one candidate, or distribute them upon two or more candidates, as he may prefer.

SEC. 5. No foreign corporation shall do any business in this State without having one or more known places of business and an authorized agent or agents in the same upon whom process may be served.

SEC. 6. No corporation shall engage in any business other than that expressly authorized in its charter, nor shall it take or hold any real estate except such as may be necessary and proper for its legitimate business.

SEC. 7. No corporation shall issue stocks or bonds except for money, labor done, or money or property actually received, and all fictitious increase of stock or indebtedness shall be void. The stock and indebtedness of corporations shall not be increased except in pursuance of general law, nor without the consent of the persons holding the larger amount in value of the stock first obtained at a meeting to be held after sixty days' notice given in pursuance of law.

SEC. 8. Municipal and other corporations and individuals invested with the privilege of taking private property for public use shall make just compensation for property taken, injured, or destroyed by the construction or enlargement of their works, highways or improvements, which compensation shall be paid or secured before such taking, injury, or destruction. The General Assembly is hereby prohibited from depriving any person of an appeal from any preliminary assessment of damages against any such corporations or individuals made by viewers or otherwise; and the amount of such damages in all cases of appeal shall, on the demand of either party, be determined by a jury, according to the course of the common law.

SEC. 9. Every banking law shall provide for the registry and countersigning, by an officer of the State, of all notes or bills designed for circulation, and that ample security to the full amount thereof shall be deposited with the auditor general for the redemption of such notes or bills.

SEC. 10. The General Assembly shall have the power to alter, revoke or annul any charter of incorporation now existing and revocable at the adoption of this Constitution, or any that may hereafter be created, whenever, in their opinion it may be injurious to the citizens of this Commonwealth, in such manner, however, that no injustice shall be done to the corporators. No law hereafter enacted shall create, renew or extend the charter of more than one corporation.

SEC. 11. No corporate body to possess banking and discounting privileges shall be created or organized in pursuance of any law without three months' previous public notice, at the place of the intended location, of the intention to apply for such privileges, in such manner as shall be prescribed by law, nor shall a charter for such privilege be granted for a longer period than twenty years.

SEC. 12. Any association or corporation, organized for the purpose, or any individual, shall have the right to construct and maintain lines of telegraph within this State, and to connect the same with other lines, and the General Assembly shall, by general law of uniform operation, provide reasonable regulations to give full effect to this section. No telegraph company shall consolidate with, or hold a controlling interest in, the stock or bonds of any other telegraph company owning a competing line or acquire, by purchase or otherwise, any other competing line of telegraph.

SEC. 13. The term "corporations," as used in this article, shall be construed to include all joint stock companies or associations having any of the powers, or privileges of corporations, not possessed by individuals or partnerships.

ARTICLE XVII.
RAILROADS AND CANALS.

SEC. 1. All railroads and canals shall be public highways, and all railroad and canal companies shall be common carriers. Any association or corporation, organized for the purpose, shall have the right to construct and operate a railroad between any points within this State, and to connect at the State line with railroads of other States. Every railroad company shall have the right with its road to intersect, connect with, or cross, any other railroad; and shall receive and transport each the other's passengers, tonnage, and cars, loaded or empty, without delay or discrimination.

SEC. 2. Every railroad and canal corporation organized in this State, shall maintain an office therein, where transfers of its stock shall be made, and where its books shall be kept for inspection by any stockholder or creditor of such corporation, in which shall be recorded the amount of capital stock subscribed, or paid in, and by whom, the names of the owners of its stock, and the amounts owned by them, respectively, the transfers of said stock, and the names and places of residence of its officers.

SEC. 3. All individuals, associations, and corporations shall have equal right to have persons and property transported over railroads and canals, and no undue or unreasonable discrimination shall be made in charges for, or in facilities for, transportation of freight or passengers within this State, or coming from or going to any other State. Persons and property transported over any railroad, shall be delivered at any station, at charges not exceeding the charges for transportation of persons and property of the same class, in the same direction, to any more distant station; but excursion and commutation tickets may be issued at special rates.

SEC. 4. No railroad, canal or other corporation, or the lessees, purchasers, or managers of any railroad or canal corporation, shall consolidate the stock, property, or franchises of such corporation with, or lease or purchase the works, or franchises of, or in any way control any other railroad or canal corporation, owning, or having under its control, a parallel or competing line; nor shall any officer of such railroad or canal corporation act as an officer of any other railroad or canal corporation, owning, or having the control of a parallel or competing line; and the question whether railroads or canals are parallel or competing lines shall, when demanded by the party complainant, be decided by a jury as in other civil issues.

SEC. 5. No incorporated company doing the business of a common carrier shall, directly or indirectly prosecute or engage in mining or manufacturing articles for transportation over its works ; nor shall such company, directly or indirectly, engage in any other business than that of common carriers, or hold or acquire lands, freehold or leasehold, directly or indirectly, except such as shall be necessary for carrying on its business; but any mining or manufacturing company may carry the products of its mines and manufactories on its railroad or canal not exceeding fifty miles in length.

SEC. 6. No president, director, officer, agent, or employé of any railroad or canal company shall be interested, directly or indirectly, in the furnishing of material or supplies to such company, or in the business of transportation as a common carrier of freight or passengers over the works owned, leased, controlled, or worked by such company.

SEC. 7. No discrimination in charges or facilities for transportation shall be made between transportation companies and individuals, or in favor of either, by abatement, drawback, or otherwise, and no railroad or canal company, or any lessee, manager or employé thereof, shall make any preferences in furnishing cars or motive power.

SEC. 8. No railroad, railway or other transportation company, shall grant free passes, or passes at a discount, to any person except officers or employés of the company.

SEC. 9. No street passenger railway shall be constructed within the limits of any city, borough or township, without the consent of its local authorities.

SEC. 10. No railroad, canal or other transportation company, in existence at the time of the adoption of this article, shall have the benefit of any future legislation by general or special laws, except on condition of complete acceptance of all the provisions of this article.

SEC. 11. The existing powers and duties of the auditor general in regard to railroads, canals, and other transportation companies, except as to their accounts, are hereby transferred to the secretary of internal affairs, who shall have a general supervision over them, subject to such regulations and alterations as shall be provided by law; and in addition to the annual reports now required to be made, said secretary may require special reports at any time upon any subject relating to the business of said companies from any officer or officers thereof.

SEC. 12. The General Assembly shall enforce by appropriate legislation the provisions of this article.

ARTICLE XVIII.

FUTURE AMENDMENTS.

SEC. 1. Any amendment or amendments to this Constitution may be proposed in the Senate or House of Representatives; and if the same shall be agreed to by a majority of the members elected to each house, such proposed amendment or amendments shall be be entered on their journals with the yeas and nays taken thereon, and the secretary of the Commonwealth shall cause the same to be published three months before the next general election, in at least two newspapers in every county in which such newspapers shall be published; and if, in the General Assembly next afterwards chosen, such proposed amendment or amendments shall be agreed to by a majority of the members elected to each house, the secretary of the Commonwealth shall cause the same again to be published in the manner aforesaid; and such proposed amendment or amendments shall be submitted to the qualified electors of the State in such manner and at such time, at least three months after being so agreed to by the two houses, as the General Assembly shall prescribe; and, if such amendment or amendments shall be approved by a majority of those voting thereon, such amendment or amendments shall become a part of the Constitution; but no amendment or amendments shall be submitted oftener than once in five years. When two or more amendments shall be sudmitted they shall be voted upon separately.

Adopted at Philadelphia, on the third day of November, in the year of our Lord one thousand eight hundred and seventy-three.

JOHN H. WALKER,
Attest: D. L. IMBRIE, *President.*
Chief Clerk.

APPENDIX.

A Congress comprises all the sessions held in the two years of a representative's term. Usually two sessions are held. The long session begins on the first Monday in December of odd years and adjourns at its own pleasure. The short session begins on the first Monday in December of the even years and continues until noon of the 4th of March following.

"Original juristiction is the right to hear and determine a cause in the first instance."

If a suit is begun in a certain court then that court has *original* jurisdiction.

In cases in which a suit is taken from a lower to a higher court, the higher court has appellate jurisdiction.

An ex post facto law is one which makes a crime punishable which was not so when committed. An increase of punishment would also be an ex post facto law with respect to crimes committed before it was passed.

SALARIES OF GOVERNMENT OFFICIALS OF THE
UNITED STATES.

President of United States, $50,000.
Vice-President of United States, $8,000.
Cabinet officers, $8,000.
Speaker of House of Representatives, $8,000.
United States Senators, $5,000.
Representatives in lower house, $5,000.
Chief Justice, $10,500.
Associate justices, $10,000.

Ministers to Great Britain, France, Germany, Russia, $17,500 each.

Ministers to Austria, Brazil, China, Italy, Japan, Mexico, Spain, $12,000 each.

Ministers to Central America, Chili, Peru, $10,000 each.

The President's private secretary, $3,250.

Clerk to each Senator, $1,000.

Sergeant-at-arms of the Senate, $4,320.

Sergeant-at-arms of House of Representatives, $4,000.

Librarian of Congress, $4,000.

Governors of territories, $2,600.

Circuit judges, $6,000.

District judges, nearly all, $3,500; some get $4,000, and one judge in California, $5,000.

Reporter of Supreme Court, $5,700.

Clerk of Supreme Court, $6,000.

Each of the five judges of the Court of Claims, $4,500.

ACQUISITION OF TERRITORY.

a. Louisiana purchase, made in 1803 by the Monroe treaty and for which we paid to France the sum of $15,000,000. The total cost, however, was $27,267,621.98, equal to three and three fifth cents per acre. The purchase contained 1,182,752 square miles.

b. The Florida purchase, made in 1819, by treaty between the United States and Spain, secured 59,268 square miles; at a total cost of $6,489,768, or seventeen and one tenth cents per acre.

c. The Mexican cession was confirmed to the United States by the treaty of Guadaloupe Hidalgo in 1848, by which the territory now comprising California, Nevada, Utah, the greater part of Arizona, and New Mexico, and a part of Colorado, with a total area of 522,568 square miles, was transferred to the United States, at a cost of $18,000,000, or five and one fourth cents per acre.

d. By the Gadsden purchase in 1853 the Mesilla valley was acquired from Mexico at a cost of $10,-000,000. It comprises 45,535 square miles, and cost more per acre than any other purchase made by the United States—thirty-four and three tenths cents per acre being paid.

e. Alaska was purchased from Russia in 1867 by the Seward treaty, This area covers 577,390 square miles, and cost $7,200,000, or one and nineteen twentieths cents per acre.

JUDICIAL DEPARTMENT OF THE UNITED STATES.

The judicial department of the United States consists of:

a. One Supreme Court which is always held at Washington.

b. Nine circuit courts comprised as follows :

(1) Maine, New Hampshire, Massachusetts, Rhode Island.

(2) Vermont, Connecticut, New York.

(3) New Jersey, Pennsylvania, Delaware.

(4) Maryland, West Virginia, North Carolina, South Carolina.

(5) Georgia, Florida, Alabama, Mississippi, Louisiana, Texas.

(6) Ohio, Michigan, Kentucky, Tennessee.

(7) Indiana, Illinois, Wisconsin.

(8) Minnesota, Iowa, Missouri, Kansas, Arkansas, Nebraska, Colorado.

(9) California, Oregon, Nevada.

c. Sixty-four district courts as follows :

(1) Three each in Alabama, New York, Texas.

(2) Two each in Arkansas, Florida, Georgia,

Illinois, Michigan, Mississippi, Missouri, North Carolina, Ohio, Pennsylvania, Tennessee, Virginia, Wisconsin.

(3) One each in all other States.

Posse Comitatus—Literally, to have the power of the county. People called to the assistance of the sheriff whenever he is resisted, and unable to execute the orders of court, or to suppress riot or lawlessness within the territory over which he has jurisdiction.

Veto—When the Governor or President refuses to sign a bill that has passed both branches of the legislative body he is said to veto it. It cannot then become a law unless passed again by a two thirds majority of each house. He usually sends a message to the house where it originated stating his reasons for refusal to sign.

www.ingramcontent.com/pod-product-compliance
Lightning Source LLC
Chambersburg PA
CBHW030255170426
43202CB00009B/757